Merry Christmas

Catherine McKinnon
and
Don Harron —

Rest ye merry!

ISBN 0-7725-1899-8

PUBLISHED IN 1991 BY
GODDARD-ZAXIS PUBLISHING INC.
489 KING STREET WEST
TORONTO, ONTARIO
CANADA M5V 1K4

ART DIRECTION: KELLY MICHELE DE REGT

Printed and bound in Hong Kong by Book Art Inc., Toronto

The authors and publisher would like to thank the following for permission to reprint the various works that appear in *Keeping a Canadian Christmas.*

CHRISTMAS IN THE BAY, from *You May Know Them as Sea Urchins Ma'am*, by Ray Guy © 1975. Reprinted by permission of Breakwater Books Limited, St. John's, Newfoundland.

CHRISTMAS CAPERS, adapted from *Bread and Molasses*, by Andy Macdonald © 1976. Reprinted by permission of Stoddart Publishing Co. Limited, Don Mills, Ontario.

HOODOO McFIGGIN'S CHRISTMAS, from *Literary Lapses*, by Stephen Leacock. Used by permission of the Canadian Publishers, McClelland & Stewart, Toronto.

THE PHANTOM DOG TEAM, from *Green Woods and Blue Waters*, by Harry Paddon. © Copyright Harry Paddon. Reprinted by permission of Breakwater Books Limited, St. John's, Newfoundland.

YES, SANTA, THERE IS A VIRGINIA, from *Needham's Inferno*, by Richard J. Needham © 1966. First published by Macmillan of Canada, a Divison of Canada Publishing Corporation. Reprinted by permission of the author.

AN ORANGE FROM PORTUGAL, from *The Other Side of Hugh MacLennan*, by Hugh MacLennan © 1978. Reprinted by permission of Macmillan of Canada, a Division of Canada Publishing Corporation.

IT'S NOT THE CARD, IT'S THE THOUGHT, adapted from *Whirligig*, by Ernest Buckler © 1977. Used by permission of the Canadian Publishers, McClelland & Stewart, Toronto.

THE NIGHT BEFORE CHRISTMAS IN NEWFOUNDLAND, by Bob Youden © 1984. Reprinted by permission of the publisher, Al Clouston.

SOMEDAY, by Drew Hayden Taylor © 1990. Reprinted by permission of the author.

A VOICE FOR CHRISTMAS, from *Jake and the Kid*, by W. O. Mitchell © 1961. Reprinted by permission of Macmillan of Canada, a Division of Canada Publishing Corporation.

A VERY MERRY CHRISTMAS, from *Morley Callaghan's Stories*, by Morley Callaghan © 1959. Reprinted by permission of Macmillan of Canada, a Division of Canada Publishing Corporation.

"GATHERING AT THE MEETING HOUSE," pages 76-77, is reproduced by permission of the artist, Peter Etril Snyder.

LET IT BE KNOWN TO ALL PEOPLE EVERYWHERE

that Don, Catherine, André and the various other creators of

this book wish to extend to their many friends, family members,

neighbours and well-wishers everywhere the best of this and

other Christmas seasons; and so to that end we acknowledge the

kindness and help of the following: Don Ast; Jim Bennet; Father

Francis Bolger; Kate Butler; Holly Carroll; Juliette Cavazzi;

Château Lake Louise; Christmas at Whistler; Mary Crane;

James E. Dale; Kelly Michele de Regt; Julia Drake; Eddie Dunn;

Durlacher Hof Pension, Whistler, B.C.; Doug Field; Ben Gallant;

Pierre and Joey Gallant; Tommy, Anita and Philip Gallant; Peter

Goddard; Catherine Griffin; Joan Gross; Heidi Hallett; Barbara

ACKNOWLEDGEMENTS

Hamilton; Aunt Jeanne Harper; Kelley Harron; Chris Hoy; Bill

Hughes; Norman and Dixie Jewison; Karen Oxley Kennedy;

Murray Kimber; Sister Helen Klute; Paul Knoetze; Fred and

Oolani Koman; Christina Lavoie; Mona Leduc; Roland and

Marie-Thérèse Lévesque; Gerry Leys; Doug Macdonald; Kevin

MacLelland; Fred Mangallon; Brandi Martin; Nancy Mazeika;

Jack McIver; Peggy McKee; the late Helen McKinnon; René

McKinnon; Marie-Claude Michaud; Tom Michaud; National

Ballet of Canada; Aunt Lillian O'Brien; Elizabeth Paul; Marie-

Pier Picard; Gordon Pinsent; Christopher Plummer; Sonya

Procenko; Stephen Quinlan; Patrician Anne McKinnon and Jack

Rae; Jean and Larry Rashid; Brian Rochford; Mona Rossignol;

Peter Etril and Marilyn Snyder; Edna Staebler; The Santa Claus

Parade; The Spirit of Christmas, Banff; Betty Thomson; Mary

Ellen and John Tomporowski; Lois and Robert Walker; Diana

Waltman; Charles and Lynn Watson.

 *THE ICY BOW RIVER*
WINDS PAST CASTLE
MOUNTAIN IN ALBERTA'S
BANFF NATIONAL PARK.
INDIAN LEGEND SAYS
THE MOUNTAIN'S PEAK IS
HOME TO THE CHINOOK,
THE WINTER WIND THAT
WARMS THE FOOTHILLS
AND THE PRAIRIES

CONTENTS

PREFACE

KA-WUMPF! Our big front door banged shut and I could feel the vibrations on the floor of my workroom directly above. Catherine was home and in a bad mood. Foolishly, for it is not my wont, I attempted to get to the heart of the matter. She was still banging shut doors and cupboards when I entered the kitchen.

"What's wrong?"

"Nothing . . ." That's what Catherine always says when she's really upset. Had I been more sensitive, I would have realized that what was bothering her was the same thing that was nagging at me. Christmas.

The birthday of our Lord had turned into an occasion to be endured, not enjoyed: something to be got past, out of the way and over with. Ogden Nash has a poem that states that roses are things of which Christmas is not a bed of them. Boxing Day sales were replacing December 25 as the really anticipated and longed-for event. What a dismal, cynical prospect as we approached once again the most important holy day of our year!

That year I had succumbed completely to the Boxing Day mania. I am notorious within my family for starting my shopping on December 23, and this particular year most of my purchases had been gift certificates, so that my nearest and dearest could make their own finicky choices. My scheme was not a success.

But my wife's giving up on Christmas was something I had never considered. Catherine has always been the keeper of the flame of our Christmas traditions. The tree must be purchased in the week of the twenty-fifth, trimmed as close to Christmas Eve as possible and taken down on January 6, not the day before nor the day after. I think it was the black Christmas tree that marked the turning point, the nadir of our seasonal disillusionment. It was displayed on a TV news show as part of "current trends in Yuletide fashions." Set off in stark contrast with gold and silver ornaments, it was considered chic and a definitive statement of . . . what? The Age of Nihilism, which followed the Age of Greed, which was preceded by the Age of Narcissism?

Christina Rossetti has the best reply to all this:

WHAT CAN I GIVE HIM

POOR AS I AM?

IF I WERE A SHEPHERD

I WOULD BRING A LAMB,

IF I WERE A WISE MAN

I WOULD DO MY PART . . .

YET WHAT CAN I GIVE HIM?

GIVE MY HEART.

To my wife, that black imitation fir was the darkness that preceded the dawn of renewed Christmas spirit in our immediate family. It gave her a determination to go back to the traditions that made Christmas meaningful for all of us in the first place. As Northrop Frye once said, we begin to see the truth by not forgetting.

Hence this book.

PART 1

THE EARLIEST YEARS

ATHERINE CALLS JANUARY 6 LITTLE Christmas. I knew it was called Epiphany, but until I did some digging around, I didn't realize that January 5 was celebrated as Christmas Eve in Greek Orthodox churches. And some orthodox Armenians celebrate Christmas Eve on January 17. Scholars think Christ was born about 6 BC, which sounds like a contradiction. Our Lord must have been born before BC, though, because the King Herod who tried to kill Him at birth died in 4 BC.

Julius Caesar created a new calendar in 46 BC and set the date of the New Year as January 1. Until that time, the New Year had begun with the vernal equinox, on or after March 21, and was a time for feasting and exchanging gifts.

Caesar's calendrical reforms didn't catch on immediately with the rest of Europe. It was the French who were the first to come on board, and they waited until AD 1564. The spring holiday then became a kind of mockery of the old celebration, and instead of exchanging gifts, people played tricks on each other. That's how the old New Year's Day became April Fools' Day (also known as All Fools' Day).

The Scots adopted Caesar's calendar in 1600, although by that time it was called the Gregorian calendar. Until 1752, the English were still whooping it up on New Year's sometime between March 21 and April 1.

The actual celebration of Christ's birthday didn't happen until halfway through the fourth century, AD 336 to be exact. It was originally celebrated on January 6, but most churches during the course of the fourth century changed it to December 25. That time of year had been an excuse for a festive occasion many centuries earlier. The winter solstice, on

or near December 21, the longest night of the year, heralds the rebirth of the sun and an occasion for living it up.

This happened mostly in the northern part of the world, where the presence of the sun is so vitally important; rain was worshipped in southern climes. Perhaps this need to create warmth in the midst of cold came as early as the invention of fire, the hot light that staves off the darkness of winter. Flame, like red, is a cheerful colour.

Even the Inuit, in pre-Christian times, had a festival for the winter solstice. They built several igloos together and cut away the inside walls to make a kind of snow cathedral with a five-metre-high roof for their drum dances.

The Norsemen worshipped their god Odin by burning a Yule log, and the feast lasted as long as it continued to burn, which could take up to two weeks! A branch of it was kept to light the following year's log. The wood of the Yule log brought luck to the household that kept it burning. Viking traditions persist in England to this day. Their descendants in the Shetland Islands up until recently burned a Viking ship to mark Christmas. Maybe they still do, but I can't imagine they have ships to burn.

Yuletide was originally celebrated at the end of summer, but the time for it got moved later and later into the fall season. Without refrigeration, berries must be eaten when they are ripe, and feasting must come before dieting becomes compulsory. Some animals in the Northern Hemisphere still follow this cycle of gorging then fasting through hibernation.

Primitive peoples worshipped light and feared darkness, and as the winter solstice approached, there was a feeling that the sun might be extinguished altogether. Even the Hindu *Upanishads*, written hundreds of years before Christ's birth, called the Lord Brahma the Light Imperishable That Drives out the Darkness. The Zoroastrians of Persia worshipped a god of light called Ahura Mazda. The Magi who followed the light of a star to a manger in Bethlehem were probably Zoroastrian astrologer-priests. The Jewish celebration of Hanukkah, with its menorah of candles, is a Festival of Light. For Christians, Jesus is the Light of the World; in the words of the children's hymn, "Jesus bids us shine with a pure, pure light, like a little candle burning in the night." All of this to stave off the darkness that surrounds us at this time of year.

PART 2

By Ray Guy

Christmas in the Bay

I N THE LAST WEEK OF ADVENT THE HOUSE SMELLED

LIKE A FOREST. BEHIND THE KITCHEN STOVE, STACKED AS NEATLY

AS BOOKS ON LIBRARY SHELVES, WAS A WALL OF

FIREWOOD. SOME JUNKS OF DRY AND WEATHERED RAMPIKES BUT

MOST OF SAPPY SPRUCE AND BALSAM FIR WITH

TURPENTINE BLADDERS AND GREEN TWIGS STICKING OFF.

The heat from the stove brought out the smell. Out in the porch there were firewood reinforcements. The woodbox was full; it was piled high and at both ends.

In all, there was enough firewood in the house and ready to do, along with a few scuttles of coal, for twelve days and twelve nights.

Some say the artificial Christmas trees are disappointing because there's no smell on them. In the mid-nineteen-forties, Christmas trees were still uncommon out around the bay but you wouldn't have noticed the smell of one anyway for the aroma off the twelve-days' supply of firewood.

The kitchen stove was the only source of heat in the house. It was allowed to die out at night and was relit each morning with splits and shavings.

Indeed, people passed every night of the winter in uninsulated houses with no fire, no storm windows. If it was ten degrees out of doors, by morning it could be ten degrees in the bedrooms.

They kept warm on mattresses stuffed with the feathers and

Considering the circumstances, Christmas then was heroically defiant, positive and optimistic

down of chickens and wild birds, covered over with quilts and comforters stuffed with wool.

Now we have a fuel crisis and great countries are plunged into distress because thermostats have to be turned down to sixty-eight degrees.

Christmas lasted a whole twelve days then. It was the most remarkable celebration of the year. Even weddings did not come close to it.

Everything possible was done to see that work was cut to a bare minimum during these twelve days. Enough firewood was in and the water-barrels in the porch brimmed full of water from the well.

All the laundry, baking, scrubbing, butchering, brewing, polishing, mending, patching and cleaning had been done until seven days into the New Year.

There was little work to be done in Christmas except to shovel the drifts from the door in the morning and feed the hens, sheep, horse and cow in the evening.

Christmas now is a glorified weekend. People then apparently determined to give themselves the whole twelve days because they knew they needed it. It was not coincidence that a hard-working people gave themselves the longest break of the year at such a time.

It is the darkest time of the year; the long, hard winter stretches ahead. So why not shatter the darkness and gloom

with a glorious bash that was the highlight of the year in those times and would be impossible to achieve in today's society.

Considering the circumstances, Christmas then was a heroically defiant thing, a blaze of light hurled by puny men against the longest night; a brazen riotous celebration to say that in the midst of darkness the Saviour was born and the people would live through the cold, both in body and soul.

It was a most positive and optimistic thing.

During those twelve days people would do things they wouldn't dream of doing during the rest of the year.

For instance, they got drunk. Well not "drunk" as the word means today, but they had "a drop in". Respectable, stern, sober pillars of the church had to be helped home once or twice through Christmas along the slippery roads by boys holding them up and they beaming happily and misplacing their feet as if they were the very lords of misrule.

But people said, "Oh, well, 'tis Christmas, you know." It was just not done to even recall in July that these stern old greyhairs had danced so wild in the reels on St. Stephen's Day.

The turkey wasn't invented yet but there were rabbits in the bakepot and turrs in the oven. There were fowls stewed tender with onions and stuffing and the carcass of a lamb or pig hanging down in the store over the water where it would keep.

There were ducks and geese and venison and salt water birds. There were herring and potatoes and bread. There was jam yesterday, today and tomorrow. There were candies and brew and brandy from St. Peter's.

And there was rum washed out of rum puncheons and wine in bottles from Madeira. There was lots of church, and the poles with the kerosene lamps on them on both sides of the aisle were wrapped in evergreen boughs and tissue-paper roses.

If there was snow there was lots of coming down hills on all sorts of slides in the nights when the moon was bright as day.

There were all the men and boys playing football with a blown-up pig's bladder covered over and stitched with sail canvas.

There was everything. There was everything for everybody.

And the old ladies said, well, perhaps they would, since it was Christmas, have just a little stain, just a little small stain for their stomach's sake and . . . Oh, my it made them right giddy-headed, ha, ha.

On New Year's night the church bell would ring and all the guns fired off just like at a wedding because, I suppose, they were taking another New Year for better for worse, for richer or poorer, in sickness and in health. . . .

And Old Christmas Day was almost as good as Christmas Day except a little smaller and it was said you could go up to the stable at twelve o'clock in the night and hear the beasts talk.

Then that was it for another year and it was a good thing.

PART 3

THE UNCONQUERED SON

➤ AT ST. MARY'S
CHURCH IN INDIAN RIVER,
PRINCE EDWARD ISLAND,
FATHER ARTHUR
PENDERGAST AND AN
ALTAR BOY, JUSTIN
CAMPBELL, PREPARE
FOR SERVICE. THIS
MAGNIFICENT, 600-SEAT
CHURCH, DESIGNED
BY THE ARCHITECT
WILLIAM HARRIS, WAS
BUILT IN 1909

I**N MOST OF THE WORLD, FRESH FOOD IS SCARCE** during the month of December. For primitive peoples, it was a time to hunt for game, or they would slaughter their livestock when the snows made it difficult to find food. They offered the animals to the gods and then made a feast of the burning sacrifices. Rituals of sympathetic magic were induced to make sure that the crops would return. One of the reasons a boar's head had such a prominent place in these feasts was because the primitive people learned how to till the soil by watching a wild boar dig for roots with its tusks. Later, of course, the wild boar became known for its ability to destroy crops.

Liquor was often involved in the ceremony of the harvest feast; fermentation represented to the primitive growers a kind of magic. Even the cattle were encouraged to get drunk, and wine was poured on the roots of fruit trees to encourage growth. Like the cattle of primitive tribes, their gods had horns and hooves, as did their shamans and witch doctors. These horned gods were powers for good; it was Christianity that turned them into devils.

The birthday of the unconquered sun of pagan times became with Christianity a celebration of the birth of the "Unconquered Son," Jesus, the little baby who bloomed in the midst of the harshness of winter.

The evergreen is still the most persistent image of winter's festivals, a permanently summer-looking tree amid the snows, suggesting fertility and hope in the midst of sterility. The Druids were the original Green Party. Besides indulging in human sacrifice, they worshipped mistletoe, which they considered a wonder drug, a protector against disease and poison. The Druids felt that those sticky white berries cured everything, even though they were also poisonous. That's probably why Christians don't allow it in their churches. Poisonous, too, are the leaves of the poinsettia (named, incidentally, after Joel R. Poinsett, U.S. ambassador to Mexico, who brought the plant home to South Carolina in 1829). Ivy represents the soul of mankind submitting to the Lord.

The Druids hung mistletoe above their doors as a sign that old quarrels were to be forgotten. A kiss under the mistletoe became a promise of good things to come. That's probably why it got a reputation as a mild aphrodisiac that leads to indiscriminate affection.

Holly is the plant that goes to church regularly. These two plants, holly and mistletoe, signify the miracle of Christmas by bearing fruit only in winter. Holly was supposed to have magical power to protect you against witchcraft, lightning bolts and evil spirits. Its pricking leaves were reputed to have been used for Christ's crown of thorns, which is why, it's said, its yellow

berries turn red like blood. Holly is considered to be the male symbol and ivy is the female, and mistletoe, I suppose, the agent that brings them together.

The hawthorn tree also has red berries, which are supposed to wait until Christmas Day to bloom. After the Crucifixion, Joseph of Arimathea took the Holy Grail and travelled from the Holy Land to Glastonbury in England. Legends say he stuck his hawthorn staff in the ground and it sprouted leaves. I visited that enormous tree when I was spending a season with the Old Vic in nearby Bristol, and the Glastonians told me that sometimes it bursts into bloom on January 6.

The twenty-fifth of December is also the birth date of the Persian god Mithra, who came forth from a rock. A lot of mediaeval paintings of Christ's birth show it happening in a cave rather than a stable and a lot of stables in Palestine were actually clefts in the face of a rocky cliff. Giotto was the first painter to put the holy baby in a crib. St. Francis put Him in a manger and added live animals to make the first Nativity scene.

I*nuit Christmas festivities last from December 25 to 31, with gifts exchanged each day of that week. The traditional Christmas community feast consists of caribou, seal or Arctic char with tea and bannock*

➤ *SNOW BRIGHTENS THE YARD OF ST. NICHOLAS ANGLICAN CHURCH AND ITS SURROUNDING COMMUNITY OF TORBAY, A SMALL FISHING VILLAGE (POPULATION 4,000) NORTH OF ST. JOHN'S, NEWFOUNDLAND*

Like Christianity, Mithraism had baptism, a eucharist, a last trump and a kind of heaven and hell, but there was no place for women. According to this religion, women had no souls, which is probably why Christianity triumphed over Mithraism in a somewhat liberated Roman Empire.

The Romans had seven days of feasting starting December 17 called Saturnalia. It was devoted to their god Saturn, a farmer who ate his own children to cancel their plans for patricide. Despite that, Saturnalia was a time for Roman farmers to relax, stop quarrelling with their neighbours and give each other gifts.

Christians retained the custom of giving gifts at this season, despite the fact that it was discouraged by early Christian church leaders. Eventually they yielded to popular pressure and linked the gift giving to the story of the three kings bringing offerings to the Christ child, although the giving of presents was done at New Year's until the 1880s.

The Saturnalia was followed by the feast of Janus, a two-faced god who looked both ways as he swung the door open onto the New Year. The bleakness of climate at that time of year seems to create an urge to be extravagant. The feeling persists today: save up during harvest to spend at the year's end. Saturnalia was frowned on by the early church, and it may be that Christ's birthday was moved to December 25 in an attempt to dislodge the heathen holiday.

PART 4

CHRISTMAS CAPERS

BY ANDY MACDONALD

WEEKS BEFORE THE TIME FOR THE STOCKINGS to be hung, when Ma and Pa were visiting neighbours, we could read each others' minds. With Ma and Pa only a few feet out the door, Bill would take us to the hiding place under an unused darkened cupboard. We didn't go there too often as we were told it was a rat hideout and we could get a nasty bite in the dark. As we got older Bill got the nerve to check.

This one Christmas Eve, four pair of bobskates were found. There was a large pond a hundred feet from the house, an ideal place to try them. We forgot that it had been unseasonably mild for the last few days; before us lay four pair of skates. At 2 a.m. with the house in silence, we slithered out of bed like baby snakes. Almost walking on air so as not to make too much noise when our weight hit the twelfth step and it creaked, downstairs we crept. We spied our skates again, which were now sitting under our stockings, which hung on three-inch nails so that Santa could leave each of us one hundred pounds of his loot. (A claw hammer was placed near by to pull out the nails as soon as the stockings were taken down in case Pa might brush up

Bob Skates Aren't for Swimming

against them, tear off half his shirt, and ruin our Christmas.)

The skates were put on in silence. Led by Bill, we raced to the pond. Though the morning was dark we found the small path, and with a formidable thrust we all followed Bill out onto the darkened pond. The ice, about one thousandths of an inch thick, wouldn't have held a beam of light — yet here we were following Bill at breakneck speed across the pond, waist deep, half crying and half laughing until we reached the other side, a distance of two hundred feet. Taking the skates off, we tried to dry them with our shirt tails. Then, skates over our shoulders

and sock-footed, we took the land way home. There, more drying was administered in silence. The skates were placed back under our socks and off we slunk to bed.

Feeling too damp to sleep we whispered until 8 a.m. Then we heard heavy footsteps and we knew Pa was in motion. Like sweetly-behaved kids, we followed him downstairs trying to make a scene of gleeful surprise as in the old English plays. Luckily Pa fell for our act and advised us how we were to take care of our skates by drying them off thoroughly after use, not knowing we had baptized them six hours before in the pond.

OH, MY POOR DUCK

THAT FEELING OF **CHRISTMAS** FOR A CHILD IS one he'll never have again. Just to hear the word "Christmas" spoken was a thrill, even in July.

A week before Christmas we were at our best, willing to do anything for any member of the family without argument. A few days before Christmas, Pa would give each of us a dollar bill to buy something for ourselves. How we appreciated that! What great affection we had for Pa who had been so rough on us throughout the year.

Billy was the slickest of us all. He would always buy Pa a good substantial present, not with thoughts of love, but speculating on a gift from Pa that would cost much more than his. With the Christmas spirit spreading over us, we'd go to town next day to look over the toys.

Our scheme was to buy as many gifts as a dollar could buy, without taking too much of the dollar. I bought a metal duck with a winder on it. When wound the duck would flap and quack. It cost sixty-nine cents, but for the first few days it was priceless. As soon as I'd open my eyes in the morning, the duck would be on my mind. I guess I thought too much of it. The greatness of it couldn't go on forever. One morning Teedy walked on it with a pair of heavy shoes and cut off all circulation to the quack and the flap. We tried everything to repair it. I can still see the look on the duck's face, as though it were suffering pains and aches in its crushed tin body.

But Teedy had a frog, which croaked and jumped when you wound it. Nowadays, in retaliation, a brother might jump on the frog and behead it, but that never crossed my mind. I just wanted half-interest in the frog in return for the damage inflicted on my duck. Since the duck was ground-born for good, all my attentions went to the frog. It was constantly on my mind. Teedy then issued a bulletin that he would wind him twice to my once. I accepted this, and things were going wonderfully for a few days. Then one mild day in January when Teedy was nowhere in sight and snow was scarce, I figured the frog would do better outside in the wide open spaces. So I took Mr. Frog outside for his first outdoor show. I'd wind him up and watch him croak and leap. I was so interested in this marvellous frog, I forgot about eating. I devoured all his actions instead. I was thinking about my good fortune in having this frog all to myself outdoors when I saw the coal man coming with his horse and cart. I had to open the gate for him and his horse.

Seeing a horse was a real novelty; I forgot all about the frog and concentrated on the live horse, watching the way he knew where to go and what to do automatically. The coal was dumped and the horse took his round-about course to turn. I watched, spellbound by the sight of his muscular rump, while those big cart wheels, spoke by spoke, went over Teedy's frog. In seconds that shapely frog was completely round. The shock was tremendous. It was so severe that I forgot to shut the gate. I kept wondering, "What can I do to make it look like a frog?" But nothing I could do would help its condition. Soon Teedy arrived on the scene and when I presented him with the round frog, he went into a state of shock, not realizing I was just coming out of one. He cried and cried while I frantically tried to form a frog or anything out of the shambles I had adopted half of.

Eventually our sorrow spent itself, and we pooled the remainder of our dollars. We had eighty-two cents between us to shop with. That was big money in those days. Then we got a terrific idea. We decided to buy a live rabbit; in fact, the man who sold them gave us two for our money and said to take good care of them like he did. He couldn't have given them to better owners. We would have breathed for them if that were possible. Home we came with the rabbits, anxious to make them a perfect home. The white one was to be Teedy's and the brown and white one mine. Sleep meant nothing to us. We had live creatures to take care of. They ate much better than us for a while. Not having much time to make them a home before dark, we took them to an old hen-house and fixed up a temporary place for them. Ted's white rabbit was a lovely sight to see. Even to me it was the head of the party, and so we gave it the best place in the hen barn. I arranged a place for mine up over a few boards, which would do until the morning when we could make a better place.

Early next morning Ted and I went out to see our lovables. I found my brown rabbit stretched out full length. A board had fallen during the night and struck him squarely on the head. This was a rabbit punch that would have been fatal to any rabbit. Ted's rabbit was in paradise, while a calamity had fallen upon mine. We gave him a burial Pope Paul would have received. We prayed at his funeral, placed him in a box, and marched him to a special place in the garden. Ashes to ashes and dust to dust were sprinkled, and the lid softly closed over him.

We didn't mourn the rabbit's death for as long as we normally would have because we had Christmas to look forward to.

Who Can That Be under the Robe?

CHRISTMAS IN CHURCH WAS MOSTLY FOR THE rich. The reason we went wasn't the interest we had or the good it would do us, but to get the small bag of candy and apple which was presented to all. The poor crowd was never in the plays.

I know that if it hadn't been so noticeable and caused such confusion, we would have been rejected in the area of the candy and the apple also. What would happen when we came to these concerts with our buddies trying to cope with those VIPs? We would end up happier than any of the big shots' sons or daughters.

The show would open with a local girl with no desire to even smile at anyone in our class. Out she would come with some wooden pins and juggle them in a scientific way. Her mom and dad would naturally have the closest seat to the stage so that they could drink in their daughter's fantastic talent. The mother and father were on our black list and underlined, the same two having had police after us in school for picking up a few frozen apples from under an apple tree in November.

This juggling was getting monotonous for us as we had also seen her perform in Sunday school and in day school.

We were always willing to laugh at anything that cropped up in the minds of our friends just bubbling with fun. A nativity play and song would always be on the agenda. We'd seen this so much we could have played it ourselves without a teacher.

The stage grew dark and silence reigned. A very dim blue light shone on the shepherd, whom we suspected was a character named John and whose features in reality resembled a toad. We still weren't sure who the "lighted" wiseman was until a brighter light came on and we saw for certain it was John, with a long white robe, walking easily to the child in the manger to the tune of "We Three Kings of Orient Are". It wasn't long before I composed lyrics applicable to John's features, by singing to my buddies in a low whisper:

Who can that be under the robe?

Is it John or is it a toad?

Lift the robe and you will see

If it's John or a T-O-A-D.

This of course, was sung to the tune of "We Three Kings".

This Cardboard Duck Is Delicious

IT SEEMED THAT WE DIDN'T GET ENOUGH TO eat even on Christmas Day. One Christmas morning, Murray and I got an orange cardboard duck each from Santa. They had picked up a beautiful Christmas smell from the oranges in the bottom of our socks. Taking our ducks with us out to the old vacant hen-house, we smelled them every step of the way. We were determined that if the smell continued, there was nothing else to do but eat them and satisfy the craving for the smell that almost drove us wild.

Murray went at his first, starting from the head. Then I decapitated mine, and it took us twenty minutes before our toy cardboard ducks were devoured, with us savouring every morsel. It took a lot of saliva to chew up this pasteboard, but that didn't bother us as that beautiful smell lingered on even when the ducks were in our stomachs.

Now that everything edible was gone, all we had to look forward to was the same boring routine of school again.

What a let-down it was to come back to school — books and pencils in the same position you had left them before Christmas. Teachers had a different attitude towards life. Last time they were bubbling with love. Now it was the "Well, we've wasted a lot of time" kind of Scrooge attitude. I thought this wasn't right and began planning my hookey. If only the teacher had sighed after Christmas and said, "Well, darn, we have six months of school left, and I hate it as much as you." Then I might have stuck it out. But she let us know in no uncertain terms she was going to be tough — no more time to waste. I was wondering why I should put in another day of this outright nonsense.

Why should I care if sisal hemp came from the town of Sisal? I could do without sisal. Who needed wool from Argentina? All Pa had to do was go to the store and there was wool right there. Ninety-eight cents for a sweater, which if caught in the rain would require a major operation to remove.

This terrible let-down after Christmas and New Year's still haunts me today. Excitement, love, and everything that goes with it would come to a very abrupt halt.

Our tree was never taken down until nearly the middle of January, its spruce needles quite thin after being in a hot room since December 1. Ten-year-old strung popcorn would be taken off the tree and put away for the next Christmas. During hungry spells, we'd sneak up to the attic and eat the aged popcorn.

PART 5

THE FEAST OF FOOLS, WHICH OUR FOREBEARS celebrated in the Middle Ages, took a number of its customs from the Roman Saturnalia and was a time when rules were relaxed and all established authority turned upside down. Halloween was close enough to the winter solstice to be infused with the spirit of the Lord of Misrule, who reigned during the twelve days of Christmas. The Christmas revelry was a tradition of organized sauciness. In the Middle Ages there was dancing inside churches; prayer books read upside down; the crowning of an Abbot of Ninnies and a Pope of Fools; and the temporary installation of small boys as bishops. Masters imitated servants, the two sexes exchanged their modes of dress and everyone wore masks. There are faint echoes of this today in an army mess when officers serve their men Christmas dinner and in our homes when everyone pulls a cracker and puts on a foolish paper hat. I couldn't find any contemporary official sanction for cross-dressing except for mummers in Newfoundland and some Belgian dockworkers who cavort about in their wives' underwear (but this is in June).

OF MUMMERS & FOOLS

The insolent, irreverent spirit of mummery is certainly present in contemporary English pantomime, along with hints of the Roman Saturnalia and the Italian commedia del l'arte. Pantomime means "nothing is spoken," but in England it soon found its voice, and it was a comic one. Clowning with lots of topical references and cross-dressing started in the eighteenth century and continues today. The story is a well-known fairy tale hopped up with local material; the Principal Boy is a girl with gorgeous legs and the Dame is a gross caricature of a woman played by a low clown of a man. All the elements that got the Puritans upset are still rolling them in the aisles.

The practice of mumming is prevalent today in parts of Europe and the British Isles. There used to be a kind of mime play that mummers performed to earn their piece of cake and drink. The content of the mummers' plays stemmed from the Crusades, depicting a fight (really a sword dance) between a knight (usually St. George) and a Saracen (usually a Turkish knight with twirling moustachios). In some versions of this old play, the Turkish knight kills St. George, who is then brought back to life by a comic doctor or, in some versions, the Archangel Michael. How St. George, who shares the same day, April 23, with the birth date of William Shakespeare, got into the Christmas tradition, I'm not quite sure. He was an enormously popular hero figure who dies and gets resurrected like the miracle baby who was born on Christmas Day.

➤ *SHELVES OF COLOURFUL PAPIER-MÂCHÉ CLOWN HEADS AND ANIMAL COSTUMES AWAIT THEIR WEARERS PRIOR TO TORONTO'S SANTA CLAUS PARADE. THIS ANNUAL EXTRAVAGANZA IS SEEN BY MILLIONS OF TV VIEWERS AROUND THE WORLD*

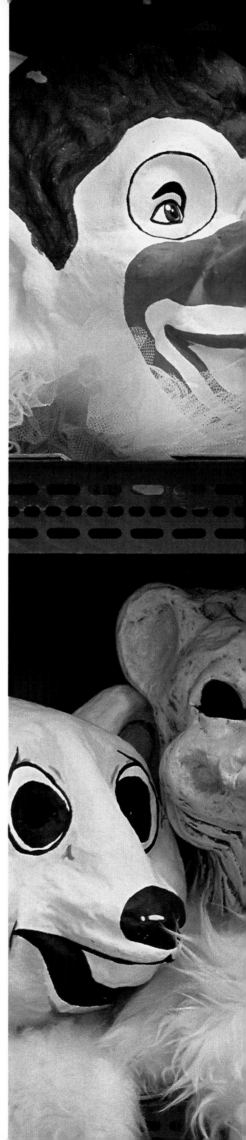

Mumming in Newfoundland is not a wandering drama festival but a bunch of masked people dressed in old clothes who invade your house and insult you while they demand food and drink. This can become raucous and uncomfortable for the hostages whose home is invaded, but usually it's a more harmless kind of buffoonery involving parents and young children all conspiring together to fool their friends about their identities.

It's more like Halloween than Christmas, except that the mask is likely a piece of cotton cloth or a burlap bag that covers your face. The mummers go from house to house disguising their voices and challenging their neighbours to guess their identities. When the correct name is guessed, the cloth comes off the face.

A favourite disguise is that of a bride or groom or even a mock clergyman. The groups start out after supper and can continue their rollicking until three or four in the morning. Sometimes the mummers are requested to sing a song or step-dance for their seasonal refreshments. Then the baking is brought out: raisin bread, partridgeberry pie and pot molasses

T he first Canadian Santa Claus Parade, sponsored by the T. Eaton Company, was held in Toronto in 1905

cake with raspberry or strawberry syrup. Cups of strong black tea are reserved for visitors, who sit around your table and share some "country meat" (bottled moose) and pork buns, not for the intruders called mummers, who prance through your house as if it were their own and are more than likely after something stronger to drink.

This custom probably grew out of the old English tradition of wassailing. Wassail, or *waes haeil*, means to be hale and hearty and was a shout directed not just at fellow humans but to the apple trees in winter to bear fruit in the coming season. Villagers went from house to house singing and getting free drinks. But there was a religious aspect to it all. Alms boxes in churches were opened the day after Christmas and distributed to the poor. Apprentices would go round to the houses of their masters, carrying with them what they called the "doll in the box." This was a wax figure of Mother Mary with her infant in her arms, a kind of portable crèche in a pottery box.

Here was the origin of the Christmas Box, which was taken around on Christmas Day, or more frequently the day after, to gather funds for priests to give to the poor. Later on, tradesmen and their apprentices would carry a box to where their customers resided, asking for the same charity for themselves. Soon there were false tradespeople, who did the same thing, accompanying it with a veiled threat, much like the kids do with their cries of "trick or treat." As the mummers would say as they knocked on doors, "Welcome, or not welcome, here I come!"

Inebriation, gluttony and loose behaviour almost put an end

the church, performed by its professional clergy, eventually turned into crude dramas portrayed by amateur tradesmen on the steps of the church.

Easter, not Christmas, was the focal point of worship in mediaeval churches. The God who was hanged upon a dead tree during the budding of spring and gave up His life so that others might have theirs was a powerful symbol that lent itself easily to drama. At first the performers were priests and nuns, but gradually subplots were added, even comic ones, until it burst open the church doors and the theatre of Rome and Athens was born again.

Eventually craft guilds would take various Bible stories as their own public domain. They took their plays off the church steps and put them on wagons and went on tour round the town. The twelve days of Christmas became a favourite theme, and the Nativity began to rival the Resurrection in popularity.

What about the weather? You may well ask. These plays were not given in December at all, but during the merry months of May and June. Appropriate stories were divided up among the various labour guilds. Carpenters got to do the story of the ark, the bakers did the Last Supper and sheepherders did the Nativity story.

Some of the plays were quite saucy. The best known of them is in the Wakefield cycle of mystery plays from the mid-fifteenth century. It's called *Secunda Pastorum*, or *The Second Shepherds' Play*. In it, a wonderful comic character called Mak steals a sheep from the shepherds who were keeping watch over their flocks by night. Actually, they weren't keeping watch, they were sleeping on the job, which is why Mak was able to cop the sheep. When his home is later invaded by these same suspicious shepherds, Mak's wife, Gill (pronounced Jill as in Mrs. John Turner), pretends the sheep is a newborn baby.

The wily Mak, sounding a bit like a parody of wicked King Herod, says that he and Gill will eat that baby if they are guilty. The ruse works. The shepherds leave, but remembering they haven't given the baby any presents, they return with a sixpence and give the baby a birthday kiss. The baby is not a pretty sight, with a long snout and eyes that are too close together. Besides that, he bleats loudly when he is kissed. The sheep is retrieved by its rightful owners, and Mak is tossed in a blanket. The shepherds go on to worship the true baby lying in a manger and bring Him gifts of a bird, a bunch of cherries and a tennis ball to play with.

It's not hard to see where these celebrations could get out of hand. Refreshments were sold, and the whole thing became a highly secular, profitable business venture. Permanent stages were built, and guilds began to take their shows out of town to other communities.

> *Oversize wreaths and a blaze of brilliant Christmas lights transform the house of Yvon and Lorraine Morneault at Baker Brook, New Brunswick. A bright winter moon adds a touch of its own*

to Christmas with the coming of the Protestant Reformation in the sixteenth century. The first Christmas tree alight with candles is credited to Martin Luther, the bringer of the Reformation, but Luther and John Calvin attacked church ritual and ceremony as being of the devil and the Christ's mass as an excuse for festive debauchery. There is some evidence to bear this out. Mummers and revellers would advance on a church with their hobbyhorses and loud pipes and drums and bells, invade its premises, interrupt the sermon, whirl up and down the aisles and end up having a drunken banquet in the churchyard.

The beginnings of theatre in the Middle Ages are mixed up in all these shenanigans. The myths and rituals that began inside

PART 6

Hoodoo McFiggin's Christmas

By Stephen Leacock

 THIS SANTA CLAUS BUSINESS IS PLAYED OUT. It's a sneaking, underhand method, and the sooner it's exposed the better.

For a parent to get up under cover of the darkness of night and palm off a ten-cent necktie on a boy who had been expecting a ten-dollar watch, and then say that an angel sent it to him, is low, undeniably low.

I had a good opportunity of observing how the thing worked this Christmas, in the case of young Hoodoo McFiggin, the son and heir of the McFiggins, at whose house I board.

Hoodoo McFiggin is a good boy — a religious boy. He had been given to understand that Santa Claus would bring nothing to his father and mother because grown-up people don't get presents from the angels. So he saved up all his pocket-money and bought a box of cigars for his father and a seventy-five-cent diamond brooch for his mother. His own fortunes he left in the hands of the angels. But he prayed. He prayed every night for weeks that Santa Claus would bring him a pair of skates and a puppy-dog and an air-gun and a bicycle and a Noah's ark and a sleigh and a drum — altogether about a hundred and fifty dollars' worth of stuff.

I went into Hoodoo's room quite early Christmas morning. I had an idea that the scene would be interesting. I woke him up and he sat up in bed, his eyes glistening with radiant expectation, and began hauling things out of his stocking.

The first parcel was bulky; it was done up quite loosely and had an odd look generally.

"Ha! ha!" Hoodoo cried gleefully, as he began undoing it. "I'll bet it's the puppy-dog, all wrapped up in paper!"

And was it the puppy-dog? No, by no means. It was a pair of nice, strong, number-four boots, laces and all, labelled, "Hoodoo, from Santa Claus," and underneath . . . "95 net."

The boy's jaw fell with delight. "It's boots," he said, and plunged in his hand again.

He began hauling away at another parcel with renewed hope on his face.

This time the thing seemed like a little round box. Hoodoo tore the paper off it with a feverish hand. He shook it; something rattled inside.

"It's a watch and chain! It's a watch and chain!" he shouted. Then he pulled the lid off.

And was it a watch and chain? No. It was a box of nice, brand-new celluloid collars, a dozen of them all alike and all his own size.

The boy was so pleased that you could see his face crack up with pleasure.

He waited a few minutes until his intense joy subsided. Then he tried again.

This time the packet was long and hard. It resisted the touch and had a sort of funnel shape.

"It's a toy pistol!" said the boy, trembling with excitement. "Gee! I hope there are lots of caps with it! I'll fire some off now and wake up father."

No, my poor child, you will not wake your father with that. It is a useful thing, but it needs not caps and it fires no bullets, and you cannot wake a sleeping man with a tooth-brush. Yes, it was a tooth-brush — a regular beauty, pure bone all through, and ticketed with a little paper, "Hoodoo, from Santa Claus."

Again the expression of intense joy passed over the boy's face, and the tears of gratitude started from his eyes. He wiped them away with his tooth-brush and passed on.

The next packet was much larger and evidently contained something soft and bulky. It had been too long to go into the stocking and was tied outside.

"I wonder what this is," Hoodoo mused, half afraid to open it. Then his heart gave a great leap, and he forgot all his other presents in the anticipation of this one. "It's a drum, all wrapped up!"

Drum nothing! It was pants — a pair of the nicest little short pants — yellowish-brown short pants — with dear little stripes of colour running across both ways, and here again Santa Claus had written, "Hoodoo, from Santa Claus, one fort net."

But there was something wrapped up in it. Oh, yes! There was a pair of braces wrapped up in it, braces with a little steel sliding thing so that you could slide your pants up to your neck, if you wanted to.

The boy gave a dry sob of satisfaction. Then he took out his last present. "It's a book," he said, as he unwrapped it. "I wonder if it is fairy stories or adventures. Oh, I hope it's adventures! I'll read it all morning."

No, Hoodoo, it was not precisely adventures. It was a small family Bible. Hoodoo had now seen all his presents, and he arose and dressed. But he still had the fun of playing with his toys. That is always the chief delight of Christmas morning.

First he played with his tooth-brush. He got a whole lot of water and brushed all his teeth with it. This was huge.

Then he played with his collars. He had no end of fun with them, taking them all out one by one and swearing at them, and then putting them back and swearing at the whole lot together.

The next toy was his pants. He had immense fun there, putting them on and taking them off again, and then trying to guess which side was which by merely looking at them.

After that he took his book and read some adventures called "Genesis" till breakfast-time.

Then he went downstairs and kissed his father and mother. His father was smoking a cigar, and his mother had her new brooch on. Hoodoo's face was thoughtful, and a light seemed to have broken in upon his mind. Indeed, I think it altogether likely that next Christmas he will hang on to his own money and take chances on what the angels bring.

PART 7

By the time the Puritans came along in Shakespeare's time, they felt that theatre, though spawned on the church steps, was Satan's handiwork. When the Civil War in England ended in victory for the Puritans, in the mid-seventeenth century, their leader, Oliver Cromwell, did his best to abolish the celebration of Christmas in England during the twenty-year run of his Commonwealth. The Puritans stomped particularly hard on the singing of carols, which were not considered hymns. These folk songs, for that's what they were, almost disappeared for the next two hundred years.

It was also illegal to either eat or make plum puddings and mince tarts on Christmas Day. There is still a law on the statute books in England saying you can't have more than three courses for your Christmas dinner! Gone also under Cromwell's republic were the usual annual subsidies, like the royal giving of alms to the poor. This caused pro-Christmas riots under Cromwell's Commonwealth, and some lives were lost in the protest. The seasonal merriment went largely underground for twenty years.

Due to the rise of Presbyterianism under John Knox, Christmas in Scotland was forbidden before the end of the sixteenth century. It has been downplayed ever since in that country in favour of celebrating Hogmanay on New Year's Eve. Some say that the word comes from a French New Year's custom, *hoguinané*, and shows the alliance between France and Scotland in Tudor times. Others say it's just a good Scottish word for oatcakes made with cheese. These are given to *wains* (young 'uns) on New Year's Eve as they wind through the streets in a long sheet looking like a Chinese dragon.

I never saw anything like that here in Canada, but I was aware even as a child of the Scots custom of "first footing." It concerns the first person to set foot in your house after midnight on New Year's Eve. It should be a dark-haired man, not a member of the family, preferably a stranger who was born feet foremost. The Wilsons lived two doors away from us, and I remember George Wilson telling me there were only two kinds of people in the world, those who were Scots and those who would like to be.

My father had dark hair, but I'm not sure which way he came into the world. I do know he was often asked to visit the Wilsons as soon as possible after midnight on New Year's Eve and to bring along a piece of bread and a lump of coal and some salt. These mundane gifts symbolized warmth and food. A branch of the evergreen was also welcome as a sign of continuing life. Money was an option, too, but this was the

Cracked & Skulls Hard Times

1930s. My mother was never asked to substitute during World War II when my dad was away, because a woman would bring bad luck. This also included the flat-footed, the lame or the squinty-eyed! The reward for fulfilling the ritual of first footing was a drink of whiskey. Some dark-haired people managed to cover a lot of houses for this very reason. My father, who was a teetotaller, swallowed his reward as if it were Buckley's cough syrup.

The censorious attitude toward December 25 was carried across the sea to the Puritan colonies of New England. To them, feasting at Christmas smacked more of the pagan Yule than the marking of Christ's birth. Town criers would warn people on their rounds not to celebrate a "merry" Christmas. It became a holiday of self-denial, more akin to Lent. The Commonwealth of Massachusetts fined anyone five shillings for feasting or for *refusing to work* on Christmas Day. But ritual's roots go deep, and undercover feasting flourished with mummers, minstrels and dancers performing in private homes; many a skull was cracked for celebrating the holy day as a holiday.

The downfall of Cromwell's Commonwealth and the return of the monarchy didn't do much to restore Christmas to its former glory. Charles II was more interested in private pleasures. In Massachusetts, Christmas Day wasn't declared a legal holiday until 1856, and the statute fining anyone five shillings for keeping Christmas on that day stayed on the books until 1959.

PART 8

THE
PHANTOM
DOG TEAM

BY HARRY PADDON

ALL SPARSELY POPULATED BACK COUNTRY AREAS HAVE THEIR GHOSTS AND LABRADOR, LIKE THE REST, HAS ITS SHARE. THE NICE THING ABOUT THE GHOSTS OF LABRADOR IS THAT THEY HAVE KEPT THE QUALITIES OF THE OLD-TIMERS OF THE ERA IN WHICH THEY ENTERED THE SPIRIT WORLD. THEY ARE A FRIENDLY, HELPFUL GROUP OF SPIRITS WITH MORE CONSTRUCTIVE THINGS TO DO THAN MERELY TO HAUNT THE LIVING AS THEIR MORE HIGHLY CIVILIZED COUNTERPARTS SEEM TO DO. INSTEAD, THEY APPEAR TO HAVE A PROTECTIVE ATTITUDE TOWARDS THEIR STILL LIVING NEIGHBORS AND DESCENDANTS.

SUCH A ONE IS THE "SMOKER" WHO, MANY TIMES, HAS STUCK HIS ETHEREAL NOSE INTO THE BATTERING BLASTS OF A LABRADOR BLIZZARD TO RESCUE A CARELESS OR UNLUCKY TRAVELLER WHO SHOULD HAVE KNOWN BETTER.

How the Smoker got his name I couldn't say unless it derives from his ability to appear and vanish like a puff of smoke, or possibly it came from the fact that his appearance always occurred on a night of smoking thick drift on the barren lands he ranged. There is no question that the many to whom he appeared, including a newly-arrived and hard-boiled Hudson's Bay man who had never heard of him, firmly believe that he did indeed come to their aid and that without his help they would surely have perished. The particular incident I wish to relate occurred some 50 years ago and, since the people involved were friends of my family, I shall take a few liberties with their names though the story shall remain theirs as they told it.

Bill and Jane Gordon's winter home lay several miles inland from their summer fishing place at Bluff Head. Chosen for the generous area of woods that had furnished logs for the comfortable house and now sheltered it from the savage winds off the rocky barrens, the winter place was an isolated spot. The nearest neighbors were two families at Rocky Cove, 15 miles

In the space of 15 minutes it was blowing a gale and in the black of the night the thickening snow blotted everything from sight in a weaving wall of wind and icy particles

across the barren, rocky neck, and it was nearly 40 miles to the trading post at Rigolet. The Neck was something to be treated with respect by winter travellers, for the way across the bare, windswept ridges was unmarked and to go astray in one of the frequent winter gales was to risk death by freezing on its pitiless miles of shelterless rocks and ice, or by plunging storm-blinded from one of its many cliffs.

A few days before Christmas Bill and Jane left home to go to Rigolet to trade their furs and bring home a few extras from the store. The two children, 12-year-old Joe and little Janet, 10, were undismayed at the prospect of being left to fend for themselves for a night or two. Joe had considered himself a man for quite some time, for he could do a man's work in the woods or the fish stage, and he had been hunting and trapping alone for a couple of winters. Janet reckoned she could look after the house as well as any woman. Joe, as he helped his father harness the dogs that morning, was rather looking forward to being the boss for a while, and it was with quite a holiday feeling that the youngsters watched the team fade into the distance as they speculated on what wonders its load might contain when it again came over the hill in two or three days.

A couple of hours on the easy going of the firm, wind-packed

snow of the ridges brought Bill and Jane to Rocky Cove where they stopped briefly for a cup of tea and a yarn with the first of their neighbors that they had not seen for two months. From Rocky Cove the way lay mostly on the ice to Rigolet and their arrival there was before sundown. Putting up at the Hudson's Bay Company's kitchen, where open house was kept for travellers, they spent the evening visiting the few households of the tiny village and the next day settled to their trading. By the time this was finished it was too late to leave Rigolet and a second night was spent in the cheery company of friends who had not been seen for months and might not again be seen for many more. It was in the graying dawn of their third day from home that Bill lashed up his load and harnessed his team for the return trip.

When the red rim of the sun turned the sea ice to a crimson plain at the purple-shadowed feet of the hills they were five or six miles on their way. The day promised to be fair as the frosty vapor from the panting breaths of the dogs hung in the still air.

They stopped again for a brief warm-up and a snack at Rocky Cove before starting the last 15 miles across the neck to home. It was with a slight feeling of unease that Bill noticed the beginning of a wispy cloud formation to the eastward as they pulled away from Rocky Cove and began the ascent to the ridges. The evening was calm and fine, however, and he reckoned that the two-hour run to home would be safely done long before any bad weather moved in.

The only worrisome thing was that his was a young team and the year-old pup he was training to be a leader seemed to have little sense. The old leader that had died last fall could have been trusted to take them home no matter how thick the weather, without deviating a whisker's length from the trail. Bill didn't quite know if he could trust the pup who always seemed to want to be told where to go. It was clouding in rapidly now and though still calm the very stillness held the menace of something waiting to pounce.

Halfway across the neck the first few snowflakes began to fall, and as darkness curtained the rocky slopes the first searching fingers of icy wind stirred the gathering powder into feathery swirls and dragged them, rustling, across the tops of the drifts. In the space of a quarter of an hour it was blowing a gale and in the black of the night the thickening snow blotted everything from sight in a weaving wall of wind and pelting icy particles. The team faltered, slowed and stopped. The young leader had no confidence in his ability to stay on the trail, and his mates shared his uncertainty. Unable to see more than a few yards, Bill began to consider the advisability of finding a hollow sheltered enough to burrow into the snow for the night. Though this would mean a risk of freezing, it might present a better chance of survival than would be offered by blundering blindly on with a very good chance of plunging over a cliff. Already the biting wind was beginning to leave little spots of frost bite on any exposed skin and it wouldn't be too long before Bill and Jane began to freeze quite badly.

Bill knew that they were still on the trail, for just there by his leader a pyramid-shaped cairn of rocks marked where the Big Brook trail came in from the north to join their own. He walked out through the team and stood by the cairn, recalling to mind the various folds in the nearby land that might offer shelter enough to permit them to get through this night. As he stood, the voice of another driver reached his ears, the voice of a man urging his team onward, and, as he looked, a team surged out of the swirling darkness. Nine black and white dogs trotted by almost near enough to touch. On the komatik behind them knelt a lone man who gestured urgently at Bill to follow before he turned again to face his team. Bill's own dogs, crazy with excitement, were already lunging into their traces and as the komatik slid by him he dropped to his seat on the load. Though the other team was a strange one to him the driver seemed to know where he was going, for he drove with the assurance of a man whose leader had been over the road before.

For an hour the two teams trotted steadily through the swirling blackness, Bill's young team straining against their heavy load to let the young leader keep his nose almost touching the stern of the leading komatik. On some of the steeper grades where the weight of their load threatened to cause them to fall behind, the black team slowed a little to let them keep up. Bill marvelled at the control the stranger had over his team, for he was travelling light and could easily run them out of sight in no time. It wasn't till a faint spark of light through the storm showed where the house lay ahead that the strange team drew ahead in a burst of speed.

Back at the house the youngsters had been having a grand time. Joe had had one day hunting ptarmigan on the ridges above the house. The second day he had harnessed up his own team of pups and gone out to the summer place, where a day on the ice foot by the open sea had yielded some of the big eider ducks that make a fine Christmas dinner. Both days, with her housework done, Janet had spent some hours fishing through the ice at the mouth of the brook, and several dozen trout and a few hundred smelt had been added to the stock of frozen fish in the bins of the storehouse. The third day they both stayed close to home, and from noon on many were the glances they took at the trail from the hills where their parents' team should appear any time now. The first twinges of anxiety began as the weather worsened at dusk. The coming of full darkness brought with it a

wind that roared off the hills and drove icy scuds of drift rattling across the window panes. The youngsters were silently thoughtful as they sat down to supper. Both hoped that the storm had struck on the other side of the neck early enough to cause their parents to stay the night at Rocky Cove.

Supper was barely over when a chorus of welcoming yelps and howls from Joe's pups brought them to their feet to stare through the windows. A team, not their father's, but a team of nine big black and white dogs, drew up to the door and stopped at a low-voiced command from the driver. Joe hastily pulled on his jacket and cap to go out and welcome the stranger and Janet watched as the dogs, in the usual fashion of a team glad to have reached the end of a hard day, rolled and rubbed their faces in the snow to rid their eyes of the accumulation of frost from their breaths. The driver stood for a moment by his komatik and coiled up his long whip as he waited for some sign from within.

As Janet watched, Joe appeared from the lean-to porch and walked into the square of lamplight from the window. The

They could easily outrun Bill's dogs but it wasn't till a spark of light through the storm showed where the house lay that the strange team drew ahead in a burst of speed

leader, a huge, powerful-looking beast, gambolled playfully toward him and Joe stooped to pull its harness off. As he reached for the leader Joe stopped and gazed unbelieving at his hands, for there was nothing between them. There on the wind-swept deck he was alone, more alone than he had ever been in his life, for nine big dogs with their driver and the big tripping komatik had vanished. Joe turned and stared back to the door, worried by what little Janet, watching from the window, might be making of this. As he reached for the latchstring an uproar of welcome again broke from his team of pups tethered in the edge of the woods. This time, as he turned to face whatever might be coming, it was his father's familiar team that trotted jauntily on to the lamp-lit deck.

The dogs crowded around Joe, rubbing their bodies against his legs, each frantic to draw his attention and be the next unharnessed. It wasn't till Joe had sorted out and coiled up the mass of sealskin traces that he approached the komatik to help his father unlash and carry in the load. As he straightened from his bent position to coil the long lash-line Bill asked, "What became of the team that came in ahead of us?"

Joe hoisted a heavy sack to his shoulder and turned toward the house. "There was no team," he answered quietly.

PART 9

THE VICTORIAN AGE

CHRISTMAS AS CANADIANS KNOW IT IS A mixture of American and English traditions. The latter are largely an invention of the Victorian age, with a hefty assist from Charles Dickens, who had an enormous influence on Christmas with the publication of one novella, *A Christmas Carol*. This was written on the rebound from his first commercial failure, the novel *Martin Chuzzlewit*. He walked the back streets of London night after night composing a ghost story about the rehabilitation of the miser Ebenezer Scrooge. It sold six thousand copies the first day of its publication, and he later performed it as a monodrama to audiences of up to thirty-five thousand people. It was the immediate popularity of *A Christmas Carol* that forced Scrooge-like factory owners to close their establishments on December 25.

This was in 1843, and the overwhelming success of his Christmas story triggered a compulsive tradition with the author. For the next few years he published a new Christmas tale almost annually (*The Chimes*, 1844; *The Cricket on the Hearth*, 1845; *The Battle of Life*, 1846; and *The Haunted Man*,

1848). None, however, achieved the popularity of *A Christmas Carol*. He included it along with readings from *The Pickwick Papers* in his final public appearance in 1870. When he died four months later, people wondered if Father Christmas had died too.

The English still call Santa Claus Father Christmas and retain for him the older-style dress of a hood and long fur robe. He and Dickens return every year without fail, although it must be said that the works of the latter stress secular altruism rather than Christian symbolism.

A Christmas tree, brought inside the house and filled with decorations, did more than Dickens to revivify the Christian nature of the holiday. It was the gift from Germany that Queen Victoria got from her beloved consort, Albert. The tree at Windsor Castle was hung with candies and sweetmeats. I have never tasted a sweetmeat, unless you include the glazed coating on a Christmas ham or the red and green cherries that are impaled upon it. Whatever they were, they were only to be eaten when the tree was finally dismantled on January 6.

PART 10

"Yes, Santa, There Is A Virginia"

By Richard J. Needham

ONCE UPON A TIME, QUITE POSSIBLY IN Toronto, there lived a 17-year-old girl named Virginia Varoom. Her parents were liberal intellectuals who had immense faith in science, reason, progress, and the perfectibility of human nature. They believed in family planning, town planning, social planning, economic planning, and planetarium planning. They did not believe in God or Santa Claus, and they brought Virginia up accordingly.

"Man has no need of myths or legends or outworn superstitions," her father would say. "He is naturally wise and good, and with the aid of science will create a world of happiness and order. By the way, Virginia, don't go out alone at night; you are the only girl on the block who has not been robbed or stabbed or most foully ravished."

Her mother would say: "We must have faith in the infinite mercy and wisdom of the State, doing everything it tells us and obediently paying it taxes which now amount to 87 per cent of your father's total income. I'm sorry they decided to liquidate all those poor Eskimoes, but no doubt the State knows what it is doing, and we are entering into an era of true democracy and social justice."

Raised in this manner, Virginia entertained no illusions about jolly old chaps in red clothes flying through the air on Christmas Eve. She got presents, to be sure, but her parents made clear they themselves had gone out and bought them. They were practical presents, too — a good pair of sensible shoes, a sensible navy-blue blazer and plaid kilt, a cultured-pearl choker, a briefcase to carry her schoolbooks, the complete works of Shakespeare.

While Virginia herself did not believe in Santa Claus, some of her school-mates did; and this infuriated her to the point where she wrote to a newspaper columnist . . . : "Dear Mr. Noodlebaum: Some of my little friends are stupid and ignorant enough to believe in Santa Claus. How can I set these creeps straight?"

He replied: "My dear young lady, I am appalled in 187 different directions to hear that anybody believes in Santa Claus. Put it this way to your chuckle-headed little friends. If they believe Santa Claus actually exists, they will find themselves believing John Diefenbaker actually exists, and then they will find themselves believing Lester Pearson actually exists; and so on up or down the line, depending how one looks at it."

Virginia was delighted, and showed the letter to her friends, and thought about it when she went to bed on Christmas Eve. What (she wondered) had her parents bought her this time? A matched set of ballpoint pens? An English-French dictionary? A blue quilted bathrobe? H. G. Wells's *Outline of History*? A heavy woollen scarf, glove, and hat set to keep out the cold?

Shortly after midnight, she was awakened by the extraordinary noise of sleigh-bells, and the extraordinary spectacle of a red-clad, white-bearded man clambering in through her window. "Ho! Ho! Ho Chi Minh!" he cried. "I am Santa-a-Go-Go, and I have brought you the presents you really want, not those creepy ones your parents are always giving you. I have brought you a cigarette-holder seventeen inches long, and a copy of the *Kama Sutra*, and a forged identity card which says you are over the legal age of 21."

Nor was that all. The dear old fellow had brought her mink eyelashes from England; black and white pony-fur knee-high boots; a Honda motor-scooter from Japan; a box of black star mouches; a white toy poodle with rhinestone collar; an appointment to have her ears pierced; a French telephone; a piece of shirt ripped from the back of Ringo Starr; a year's supply of Dr. Pepper; a modelling course; a computer to do all her homework; a lunch date with the Rolling Stones; a case of incense from Hong Kong; an appointment to have her hair done once a week by Gus Caruso; an 007 sweatshirt; credit cards with Air Canada, the Unicorn, and Sam the Record Man; a wall-to-wall sheepskin rug for her room; a cigarette partially smoked by Sean Connery; forty-eight bottles of Frosted Pink Revlon nail polish; a colour TV set with remote control; and a spring outfit specially designed for her by André Courrèges.

"And now," said Santa-a-Go-Go, "do you believe in me?" The little girl nodded her head delightedly. "In that case," he continued, "I will give you the thing you wish most of all. Whisper it into my ear." She did so. "Good as done!" he cried, and roared with laughter as he sailed off into the sky with his sleigh and reindeer.

Yes, when she went downstairs, they had vanished completely; not dead or anything awful like that; kindly old Santa-a-Go-Go had simply given them a new start in a Chinese commune, where they are very, very happy, and sing songs like *All We Want for Christmas Is To Double Our Pig-Iron Production*. Virginia thinks she might fly over to see them when she is finally satisfied with her eye make-up.

Virginia entertained no illusions about jolly old chaps in red clothes flying through the air on Christmas Eve. She got presents, to be sure, but her parents made clear they themselves had gone out and bought them. And they were practical presents, too, including the works of Shakespeare

PART 11

CHRISTMAS
AROUND THE

WORLD

RIGINALLY, THE GIFTS EXCHANGED AT Christmas were intended for the poor; now most of them remain within the bosom of the family. The bringer of gifts varies widely even within our Christian traditions. In Germany, it is Christkindl, the Christ child, a female messenger from Jesus who enters through an open window. In the United States, Christkindl changed sex and became Kriss Kringle. In Spain, it's the three kings who bring the gifts, and Spanish tots fill their own little shoes with straw or barley for the camels. In Italy, it is a witch, Befana, who delivers the gifts as a penance for her delay in following the star to Bethlehem and missing out on

everything. She brings presents, but she is still searching for the holy child. The notion of an old, jolly fat man entering and leaving by the chimney comes from the legends of witches, who achieved lift-off by jetting straight up through the fireplace on their brooms and returned the same way.

Sweden's gifts are brought by a gnome who looks like an abridged version of Father Christmas, and the children leave porridge for him. Finland has a little old man in furs, with a long white moustache but no beard. Father Frost is the Soviet way of saying Santy Claws. As far as ninety-nine and forty-four hundredths of Chinese are concerned, Christmas is the day before Mao Tsetung's birthday.

Our Santa Claus really comes from the Netherlands, where he is called Sinterklaas. However, his origin goes back to the fourth century, and the hagiographers are still trying to determine legend from fact. (Hagiographers are specialists who write about the lives of saints. Not too much call for them these days, I would think.) St. Nicholas of Myra is an enigmatic figure who

Hallmark, one of Canada's top greeting card companies, offered

sounds like he comes from a river in Cape Breton, but actually he's an Asia Minor leaguer from Turkey. He seems to have been a saint from the moment he was born; even at his mother's breast he insisted on fasting every Friday. It seems that abstinence made his heart grow fonder.

Nicholas is the patron saint of both sailors and virgins, which would seem to provoke a conflict of interest, but it turns out he saved three maids from a life of prostitution. They were the daughters of a rich man who had fallen on hard times and was determined to make up for his loss of fortune by selling his beautiful daughters into what my mother used to call "white slavery." Because it was impossible to marry them off without a dowry, St. Nicholas threw three bags of gold through their open window and saved the girls from a fate worse than death. Don't ask me where he got those three bags full, but the symbolism was not lost. By so doing, Nicholas became the patron saint of pawnbrokers. A few centuries later, another version of the story has him dropping the gold coins, sans bags, down the smoke hole of that house, and since the three girls always hung their stockings by the fire to dry, the coins ended up in them, and a tradition was born.

Nicholas also became the patron saint of Russians, Greeks,

◄ SANTA CLAUS IS MORE OFTEN SEEN DRIVING A TEAM OF NINE REINDEER, BUT FOR THIS PRACTICE RUN IN CANADA'S FAR NORTH (PREVIOUS PAGES), HE OPTED FOR A TEAM OF RACING HUSKIES

children, students, brewers and thieves. Those who saw him in the flesh record that he had a long, emaciated face, very earnest and venerable, which doesn't quite jibe with our current conception, but he did have a white beard and hair and the red robe of a bishop.

The Netherlands celebrates his arrival (by boat from Spain!) every year on December 5, not the twenty-fifth. No sirree. The Dutch don't celebrate the birthday of our Saviour with a lot of high jinks and pagan pageants. The children of Amsterdam go to the harbour to welcome their St. Nick, who rides a white horse to City Hall where he is received by the mayor. Besides this parade, there are special items in the stores for the event, and the children get presents in their wooden shoes.

Dutch settlers in North America brought their patron St. Nicholas to New Amsterdam before the town was re-named New York. By now he was a jolly, rosy-cheeked little old man with a red mitre on his snow-white head and a long pipe. Some U.S. historians say it was Washington Irving who made Kriss

But what of our hero, St. Nicholas? In 1969, he was relegated to the status of a minor saint, and veneration for him among the world's seven hundred million Roman Catholics was made voluntary rather than obligatory. That meant you could celebrate his feast day on December 6 if you wanted to, but the Vatican wasn't concerned if you didn't. The Greek Orthodox community in North America protested his demotion, and in 1972 his relics were taken from their final resting place in the town of Bari in Italy and transferred to the Greek Orthodox Cathedral in New York.

And what is Canada's contribution to the legend of St. Nicholas? Brock Chisholm. Don't tell me you've never heard of him! He was appointed deputy minister of health in 1945 after a distinguished military career as director-general of medical services for the Canadian Army. Later he became the first director-general of the World Health Organization. He was one of the first to recognize the dangers of pollution, over-population and the nuclear arms race. But he did have another

1,200 English and 500 French Christmas card designs in 1990

Kringle popular, a kind of Rip van Winkle in a red suit who gave presents to children but not to their degenerate parents. It was Irving who described him as flying over the rooftops in a wagon (I presume with horses), landing on the roof, coming down the chimney to leave the presents, having a smoke before resuming and, "laying his finger beside his nose" (Irving said it first), taking off over the treetops.

When you come right down to it, Dr. Clement Clarke Moore did more than anybody to establish our current image of Santa Claus when he wrote the poem *A Visit from Saint Nicholas* in 1822. Mind you, there's some doubt that Dr. Moore, a rather serious, pedantic scholar of oriental and Greek literature, actually wrote the thing. Some say it was a land surveyor by the name of Henry Livingston Jr. who penned it in 1804.

It established for all time that St. Nick arrives with eight flying reindeer. This was amended in 1939 when the Montgomery Ward department store created an ad campaign about a ninth reindeer with a clown's nose, an underachieving kind of deer who becomes famous by supplying Santa with his own personal fog light. In 1949 Gene Autry recorded a song based on the story of Rudolph, and a new legend was born that seems to be here to stay.

bee in his bonnet: he will be remembered by Canadians of my generation as the man who did his best to kill Santa Claus.

He said in Ottawa in 1945: "A child who believes in Santa Claus, who really and literally believes, because his daddy told him so, that Santa comes down all the chimneys in the world on the same night, has had his thinking ability permanently impaired if not destroyed. That freedom, present in all children and known as innocence, has been destroyed or crippled by local certainties, by gods of local moralities, of prejudice and hate and intolerance, frequently masquerading as love . . . gods of everything that would destroy freedom to observe and think and would keep each generation under the control of the old people, the elders, the shamans and the priests. We have swallowed all manner of poisonous certainties fed us by our parents, our Sunday and day school teachers, and others with a vested interest in controlling us."

Yes, Virginia, there was a Canadian grinch who tried to destroy the legend of St. Nicholas. But his protestations went for naught: Brock Chisholm is gone, and jolly old St. Nick is alive and well and living in Canada. As far as children are concerned, he's still busy three hundred and sixty-four days and nights of the year in that workshop close to Ellesmere Island.

PART 12

AN ORANGE
FROM
PORTUGAL

I SUPPOSE ALL OF US, WHEN WE THINK OF Christmas, recall Charles Dickens and our own childhood. So today, from an apartment in Montreal, looking across the street to a new neon sign, I think back to Dickens and Halifax and the world suddenly becomes smaller, shabbier, and more comfortable, and one more proof is registered that comfort is a state of mind, having little to do with the number of springs hidden inside your mattress or the upholstery in your car.

Charles Dickens should have lived in Halifax. If he had, that brown old town would have acquired a better reputation in Canada than it now enjoys, for all over the world people would have known what it was like. Halifax, especially a generation or two ago, was a town Dickens could have used.

There were dingy basement kitchens all over the town where rats were caught every day. The streets were full of teamsters, hard-looking men with lean jaws, most of them, and at the entrance to the old North Street Station cab drivers in long coats would mass behind a heavy anchor chain and terrify travellers with bloodcurdling howls as they bid for fares. Whenever there was a south-east wind, harbour bells moaned behind the wall of fog that cut the town off from the rest of the world. Queer faces peered at you suddenly from doorways set flush with the streets. When a regiment held a smoker in the old Masonic Hall you could see a line beginning to form in the early morning, waiting for the big moment at midnight when the doors would be thrown open to the town and any man could get a free drink who could reach the hogsheads.

For all these things Dickens would have loved Halifax, even for the pompous importers who stalked to church on Sunday mornings, swinging their canes and complaining that they never had a chance

BY HUGH MACLENNAN

to hear a decent sermon. He would have loved it for the waifs and strays and beachcombers and discharged soldiers and sailors whom the respectable never seemed to notice, for all the numerous aspects of the town that made Halifax deplorable and marvellous.

If Dickens had been given a choice of a Canadian town in which to spend Christmas, that's where I think he would have gone, for his most obvious attitude toward Christmas was that it was necessary. Dickens was no scientist or organizer. Instead of liking The People, he simply liked people. And so, inevitably, he liked places where accidents were apt to happen. In Halifax accidents were happening all the time. Think of the way he writes about Christmas — a perfect Christmas for him was always a chapter of preposterous accidents. No, I don't think he would have chosen to spend his Christmas in Westmount or Toronto, for he'd be fairly sure that neither of those places needed it.

Today we know too much. Having become democratic by ideology, we are divided into groups which eye each other like dull strangers at a dull party, polite in public and nasty when each other's backs are turned. Today we are informed by those who know that if we tell children about Santa Claus we will probably turn them into neurotics. Today we believe in universal justice and in universal war to effect it, and because Santa Claus gives the rich more than he gives the poor, lots of us think it better that there should be no Santa Claus at all. Today we are technicians, and the more progressive among us see no reason why love and hope should not be organized in a department of the government, planned by a politician and administered by trained specialists. Today we have a super-colossal Santa Claus for The Customer: he sits in the window of a department store in a cheap red suit, stringy whiskers, and a mask which is a caricature of a face, and for a month before every Christmas he laughs continually with a vulgar roar. The sounds of his laughter come from a record played over and over, and the machine in his belly that produces the bodily contortions has a number in the patent office in Washington.

In the old days in Halifax we never thought about the meaning of the word democracy; we were all mixed up together in a general deplorability. So the only service any picture of those days can render is to help prove how far we have advanced since then. The first story I have to tell has no importance and not even much of a point. It is simply the record of how one boy felt during a Christmas that now seems remote enough to belong to the era of Bob Cratchit. The second story is about the same. The war Christmases I remember in Halifax were not jolly ones. In a way they were half-tragic, but there may be some significance in the fact that they are literally the only ones I can still remember. It was a war nobody down there understood. We were simply a part of it, swept into it from the mid-Victorian age in which we were all living until 1914.

On Christmas Eve in 1915 a cold northeaster was blowing through the town with the smell of coming snow on the wind.

All day our house was hushed for a reason I didn't understand, and I remember being sent out to play with some other boys in the middle of the afternoon. Supper was a silent meal. And then, immediately after we had finished, my father put on the great-coat of his new uniform and went to the door and I saw the long tails of the coat blowing out behind him in the flicker of a faulty arc light as he half-ran up to the corner. We heard bagpipes, and almost immediately a company of soldiers appeared swinging down Spring Garden Road from old Dalhousie. It was very cold as we struggled up to the corner after my father, and he affected not to notice us. Then the pipes went by playing "The Blue Bonnets", the lines of khaki men went past in the darkness, and my father fell in behind the last rank and faded off down the half-lit street, holding his head low against the wind to keep his flat military cap from blowing off, and my mother tried to hide her feelings by saying what a shame the cap didn't fit him properly. She told my sister and me how nice it was of the pipers to have turned out on such a cold day to see the men off, for pipe music was the only kind my father liked. It was all very informal. The men of that unit — almost entirely a local one — simply left their homes the way my father had done and joined the column and the column marched down Spring Garden Road to the ship along the familiar route most of them had taken to church all their lives. An hour later we heard tugboat whistles and then the foghorn of the transport and we knew he was on his way. As my sister and I hung up our stockings on the mantelpiece I wondered whether the vessel was no farther out than Thrum Cap or whether it had already reached Sambro.

It was a bleak night for children to hang up their stockings and wait for Santa Claus, but next morning we found gifts in them as usual, including a golden orange in each toe. It was strange to think that the very night my father had left the house, a strange old man, remembering my sister and me, had come into it. We thought it was a sign of good luck.

That was 1915, and some time during the following year a boy at school told me there was no Santa Claus and put his case so convincingly that I believed him.

 STRICTLY SPEAKING, THIS SHOULD HAVE BEEN the moment of my first step toward becoming a neurotic. Maybe it was, but there were so many other circumstances to compete with it, I don't know whether Santa Claus was responsible for what I'm like now or not. For about a week after discovering the great deception I wondered how I could develop a line of conduct which would prevent my mother from finding out that I knew who filled our stockings on Christmas Eve. I hated to disappoint her in what I knew was a great pleasure. After a while I forgot all about it. Then, shortly before Christmas, a cable arrived saying that my father was on his way home. He hadn't been killed like the fathers of other boys at school; he was being invalided home as a result of excessive work as a surgeon in the hospital.

We had been living with my grandmother in Cape Breton, so my mother rented a house in Halifax sight unseen, we got down there in time to meet his ship when it came in, and then we all went to the new house. This is the part of my story which reminds me of Charles Dickens again. Five minutes after we entered the house it blew up. This was not the famous Halifax explosion; we had to wait another year for that. This was our own private explosion. It smashed half the windows in the other houses along the block, it shook the ground like an earthquake, and it was heard for a mile.

I have seen many queer accidents in Halifax, but none which gave the reporters more satisfaction than ours did. For a house to blow up suddenly in our district was unusual, so the press felt some explanation was due the public. Besides, it was nearly Christmas and local news was hard to find. The moment the first telephone call reached the newspaper offices to report the accident, they knew the cause. Gas had been leaking in our district for years and a few people had even complained about it. In our house, gas had apparently backed in from the city mains, filling partitions between the walls and lying stagnant in the basement. But this was the first time anyone could prove that gas had been leaking. The afternoon paper gave the story.

DOCTOR HUNTS GAS LEAK WITH BURNING MATCH — FINDS IT!

When my father was able to talk, which he couldn't do for several days because the skin had been burned off his hands and face, he denied the story about the match. According to modern theory this denial should have precipitated my second plunge toward neurosis, for I had distinctly seen him with the match in his hand, going down to the basement to look for the gas and complaining about how careless people were. However, those were ignorant times and I didn't realize I might get a neurosis. Instead of brooding and deciding to close my mind to reality from then on in order to preserve my belief in the veracity and faultlessness of my father, I wished to God he had been able to tell his story sooner and stick to it. After all, he was a first-class doctor, but what would prospective patients think if every time they heard his name they saw a picture of an absent-minded veteran looking for a gas leak in a dark basement with a lighted match?

It took two whole days for the newspaper account of our accident to settle. In the meantime the house was temporarily ruined, school children had denuded the chandelier in the living-room of its prisms, and it was almost Christmas. My sister was still away at school, so my mother, my father, and I found ourselves in a single room in an old residential hotel on Barrington Street. I slept on a cot and they nursed their burns in a huge bed which opened out of the wall. The bed had a mirror on the bottom of it, and it was equipped with such a strong spring that it crashed into place in the wall whenever they got out of it. I still remember my father sitting up in it with one arm in a sling from the war, and his face and head in white bandages.

Five minutes after we entered the house it blew up. This was not the famous Halifax explosion; we had to wait another year for that

He was philosophical about the situation, including the vagaries of the bed, for it was his Calvinistic way to permit himself to be comfortable only when things were going badly.

The hotel was crowded and our meals were brought to us by a boy called Chester, who lived in the basement near the kitchen. That was all I knew about Chester at first; he brought our meals, he went to school only occasionally, and his mother was ill in the basement. But as long as my memory lasts, that Christmas of 1916 will be Chester's Christmas.

He was a waif of a boy. I never knew his last name, and wherever he is now, I'm certain he doesn't remember me. But for a time I can say without being sentimental that I loved him.

He was white-faced and thin, with lank hair on top of a head that broke back at right angles from a high narrow forehead. There were always holes in his black stockings, his handed-down pants were so badly cut that one leg was several inches longer than the other and there was a patch on the right seat of a different colour from the rest of the cloth. But he was proud of his clothes; prouder than anyone I've ever seen over a pair of pants. He explained that they were his father's and his father had worn them at sea.

For Chester, nobody was worth considering seriously unless he was a seaman. Instead of feeling envious of the people who lived upstairs in the hotel, he seemed to feel sorry for them because they never went to sea. He would look at the old ladies with the kind of eyes that Dickens discovered in children's faces in London: huge eyes as trusting as bird-dog's, but old, as though they had forgotten how to cry long ago.

I wondered a lot about Chester — what kind of a room they had in the basement, where they ate, what his mother was like. But I was never allowed in the basement. Once I walked behind the hotel to see if I could look through the windows, but they were only six or eight inches above the ground and they were covered with snow. I gathered that Chester liked it down there because it was warm, and once he was down, nobody ever bothered him.

T HE DAYS WENT PAST, HEAVY AND GREY AND cold. Soon it was the day before Christmas again, and I was still supposed to believe in Santa Claus. I found myself confronted by a double crisis.

I would have to hang up my stocking as usual, but how could my parents, who were still in bed, manage to fill it? And how would they feel when the next morning came and my stocking was still empty? This worry was overshadowed only by my concern for Chester.

On the afternoon of Christmas Eve he informed me that this year, for the first time in his life, Santa Claus was really going to remember him. "I never ett a real orange and you never did neether because you only get real oranges in Portugal. My old man says so. But Santy Claus is going to bring me one this year. That means the old man's still alive."

"Honest, Chester? How do you know?" Everyone in the hotel knew that his father, who was a quartermaster, was on a slow convoy to England.

"Mrs. Urquhart says so."

Everyone in the hotel also knew Mrs. Urquhart. She was a tiny old lady with a harsh voice who lived in the room opposite ours on the ground floor with her unmarried sister. Mrs. Urquhart wore a white lace cap and carried a cane. Both old ladies wore mourning, Mrs. Urquhart for two dead husbands, her sister for Queen Victoria. They were a trial to Chester because he had to carry hot tea upstairs for them every morning at seven.

"Mrs. Urquhart says if Santy Claus brings me real oranges it means he was talkin' to the old man and the old man told him I wanted one. And if Santy Claus was talkin' to the old man, it means the old man's alive, don't it?"

Much of this was beyond me until Chester explained further.

"Last time the old man was home I seed some oranges in a store window, but he wouldn't get me one because if he buys stuff in stores he can't go on being a seaman. To be a seaman you got to wash out your insides with rum every day and rum costs lots of money. Anyhow, store oranges ain't real."

"How do you know they aren't?"

"My old man says so. He's been in Portugal and he picks real ones off trees. That's where they come from. Not from stores. Only my old man and the people who live in Portugal has ever ett real oranges."

Someone called and Chester disappeared into the basement. An hour or so later, after we had eaten the supper he brought to us on a tray, my father told me to bring the wallet from the pocket of his uniform which was hanging in the cupboard. He gave me some small change and sent me to buy grapes for my mother at a corner fruit store. When I came back with the grapes I met Chester in the outer hall. His face was beaming and he was carrying a parcel wrapped in brown paper.

"Your old man give me a two-dollar bill," he said. "I got my old lady a Christmas present."

I asked him if it was medicine.

"She don't like medicine," he said. "When she's feelin' bad she wants rum."

When I got back to our room I didn't tell my father what Chester had done with his two dollars. I hung up my stocking on the old-fashioned mantelpiece, the lights were put out, and I was told to go to sleep.

An old flickering arc light hung in the street almost directly in front of the hotel, and as I lay in the dark pretending to be asleep the ceiling seemed to be quivering, for the shutters fitted badly and the room could never be completely darkened. After a time I heard movement in the room, then saw a shadowy figure near the mantelpiece. I closed my eyes tight, heard the swish of tissue paper, then the sounds of someone getting back into bed. A fog horn, blowing in the harbour and heralding bad weather, was also audible.

After what seemed to me a long time I heard heavy breathing from the bed. I got up, crossed the room carefully, and felt the stocking in the dark. My fingers closed on a round object in its toe. Well, I thought, one orange would be better than none.

In those days hardly any children wore pyjamas, at least not in Nova Scotia. And so a minute later, when I was sneaking down the dimly lit hall of the hotel in a white nightgown, heading for the basement stairs with the orange in my hand, I was a fairly conspicuous object. Just as I was putting my hand to the knob of the basement door I heard a tapping sound and ducked under the main stairs that led to the second floor of the hotel. The tapping came near, stopped, and I knew somebody was standing still, listening, only a few feet away.

A crisp voice said, "You naughty boy, come out of there."

I waited a moment and then moved into the hall. Mrs. Urquhart was standing before me in her black dress and white cap, one hand on the handle of her cane.

"You ought to be ashamed of yourself, at this hour of the night. Go back to your room at once!"

As I went back up the hall I was afraid the noise had wakened my father. The big door creaked as I opened it and looked up at the quivering maze of shadows on the ceiling. Somebody on the bed was snoring and it seemed to be all right. I slipped into my cot and waited for several minutes, then got up again and replaced the orange in the toe of the stocking and carefully put the other gifts on top of it. As soon as I reached my cot again I fell asleep with the sudden fatigue of children.

The room was full of light when I woke up; not sunlight but the grey luminosity of filtered light reflected off snow. My parents were sitting up in bed and Chester was standing inside the door with our breakfast. My father was trying to smile under his bandages and Chester had a grin so big it showed the gap in his front teeth. The moment I had been worrying about was finally here.

The first thing I must do was display enthusiasm for my parents' sake. I went to my stocking and emptied it on my cot while Chester watched me out of the corner of his eye. Last of all the orange rolled out.

"I bet it ain't real," Chester said.

My parents said nothing as he reached over and held it up to the light.

"No," he said. "It ain't real," and dropped it on the cot again. Then he put his hand into his pocket and with an effort managed to extract a medium-sized orange. "Look at mine," he said. "Look what it says right here."

On the skin of the orange, printed daintily with someone's pen, were the words, PRODUCE OF PORTUGAL.

"So my old man's been talkin' to Santy Claus, just like Mrs. Urquhart said."

There was never any further discussion in our family about whether Santa Claus was or was not real. Perhaps Mrs. Urquhart was the actual cause of my neurosis. I'm not a scientist, so I don't know.

I *would have to hang up my stocking as usual, but how could my parents, who were still in bed, manage to fill it?*

PART 13

T<small>HE FIRST ITEM</small>

<small>ON THE</small> C<small>HRISTMAS SHOPPER'S MENU IS</small>

<small>THE</small> C<small>HRISTMAS CARD.</small> I <small>REMEMBER MANY</small>

<small>OF MY RELATIVES BUYING THEIRS IN THE</small>

B<small>OXING</small> D<small>AY SALES THE PREVIOUS YEAR.</small>

I<small>T WAS THE INVENTION OF THE PENNY</small>

<small>POSTAL SERVICE IN</small> B<small>RITAIN IN</small> 1840 <small>THAT</small>

➤ *A SAMPLING OF*
BRIGHTLY COLOURED
MUSICALS STANDS AT
ATTENTION IN CHRISTMAS
AT WHISTLER, A SPECIALTY
SHOP IN WHISTLER,
BRITISH COLUMBIA. THE
STORE SELLS ITEMS
RANGING IN PRICE FROM
$1.99 TO $50,000

WE BEGIN TO

GET READY

speeded up the exchange of cards at Christmas, if not the service itself, although it took about twenty years to really catch on. A lot of Victorians were content, like children, to create their own Christmas greetings by hand.

The big push on Christmas cards by commercial interests didn't really start until the 1860s, and in North America not until 1875. Many feel that it's beginning to fall off again. I remember when my parents' living room used to look like a greeting-card shop. A lot of the reading of Christmas cards is done by non-buying customers in card shops who don't care any more to send their very best. Perhaps facsimile machines will bring back the hunger for annual festive communication: "Merry Cholesterol and Happy New Roses!"

The very first Christmas card is a lot more recent than you might think. New Year's cards had been popular long before the first commercially printed Christmas card made its appearance. That happened in 1843 to be exact, in London (England, of course. The town of London, Ontario, in 1843 was a town of about three thousand and was still being called the Forest City).

It was the same year that Dickens published *A Christmas Carol*, and the card was criticized by temperance groups because it depicted a three-generation family raising their wine glasses in a toast to the holiday. The family is delicately hand-tinted and there are side panels in plain sepia showing charity being extended to the poor. The greeting is "A Merry Christmas and a Happy New Year to You." I'm curious about the exact wording because the English today seem to use the expression "Happy Christmas." The card cost a shilling and about a thousand of them were sold. The publisher, Henry Cole (who was also the founder of the Victoria and Albert Museum), considered the experiment a failure and did not try again.

The second Christmas card came out in 1848, with the same greeting word for word as its predecessor. The card is quite secular, showing scenes of feasting, dancing, skating and giving to the poor. The centrepiece of the card looks more like Mardi Gras than Christmas, with a male and female wrapped around each other in a dance and dressed as Columbine and Pierrot.

One of the recurring images on Christmas cards old and new is the robin, which most people think of as a harbinger of spring. The story goes that a small brown bird kept the baby Jesus warm in that cold stable by fanning the embers of a dying fire with its wings. As the embers rose into flames, the bird's chest was seared by the heat, and the robin ever after has borne a red badge of courage on its breast. Holly berries are

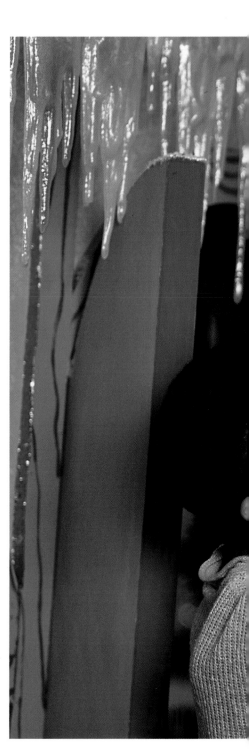

PREPARATIONS FOR TORONTO'S SANTA CLAUS PARADE REQUIRE AN AVERAGE OF 12 PEOPLE WORKING FULL TIME THROUGHOUT THE YEAR. BELOW, THE COSTUME SUPERVISOR, MARY LONGHURST (RIGHT), AND MARY WEBSTER CUT FABRIC FOR CLOWN OUTFITS; A PAINTER, IAN GREGORY, RIGHT, ADDS THE FINISHING TOUCH TO A HORSE'S HEAD

also common on Christmas cards, and their redness is a sad symbol of the drops of blood from the crown of thorns.

Riddles soon found their way into the greetings on the cards, but most of those have been relegated to the Christmas cracker, where they lie in state alongside the groaning pun. They wait for the unsuspecting sophisticate until that snapping explosion, which reveals them to the assembled revellers. I find, by the way, that that explosion works less than half the time in my incapable hands.

Charity has always been a part of the Christmas card message, but now it has become an institutionalized part of the tradition. Perhaps the card cartels aren't too pleased to have Unicef as a competitor. The gift-wrap moguls, too, must be alarmed at the environmentalists' insistence on recycling and

the use of old newspapers as a prudent, even trendy form of cover for a gift. In this I am ahead of my time. I am such a poor wrapper that my gifts, wrapped in the classified sections of newspapers, have been a standing joke in our family for years.

Now that the mailing of Christmas cards seems to be left later and later, perhaps the first ritual of the oncoming festive season is the Santa Claus Parade. I was an active spectator from my earliest years, starting on the shoulder of my father. My own shoulder has paid its dues over the years, supporting at least three children to get them a good view of Eaton's Santa Claus, the crowning glory of the procession.

The ritual almost passed into obsolescence in Toronto only a few years ago. It was saved by the intervention of former Metro Toronto chairman Paul Godfrey, who practises another faith.

Now it is seen as far away as the Soviet Union, costumed in Day-Glo colours that look more effective on television.

Travelling around last year on a book tour, I was surprised to find how many other Santa Claus parades there are across Canada. Even fairly small towns have their own homegrown, homemade parades, which are a far more important event to the locals than the one on television. In some cases there were so many citizens in the parade I wondered that there was anybody left on the sidelines to be a spectator.

If the Santa Claus Parade comes somewhere before the Grey Cup, then surely the next phase of the worship of Christmas arrives with the beginning of Advent, the first Sunday after November 26. That's when some children receive calendars that have all kinds of windows and holes in tree branches labelled with the date on which they are to be opened to reveal their secret message or hidden piece of chocolate. Perhaps the original idea was to get a secret little gift ahead of time, much like the practice of the Jewish Festival of Lights, Hanukkah,

I n a typical year, more than 8,000 Canada Post volunteers answer some 785,000 letters to Santa. The letters, from children across Canada and other parts of the world, are responded to in more than a dozen languages, including Russian, Braille, Chinese and Lithuanian

where a child receives one present a day for eight days. What a sensible arrangement, instead of having your child confused and crazy all in one frantic morning.

Quite frankly, I'm confused about the origin of the Christmas wreath. Is it a gentler version of the crown of thorns or is it more pagan, reminiscent of what the Druids wore around their heads as they committed human sacrifice? All I know is that my wife is a nut about making her own Christmas wreaths, and we have several of them outside our house, at doors front, side and back. One year Catherine made a wreath composed entirely of hard candies, which gradually disappeared one by one, or even quicker, in the weeks before Christmas.

One pre-Christmas ritual I miss is looking through the toy section of a department store catalogue. About twenty years ago the Musson Book Company published a replica of the 1901 T. Eaton Company catalogue, which boasted toy wheelbarrows with sheet steel bodies painted red with black striping and steel wheels and axles. The price? Forty cents each.

But before we rush off to Toyland, it's time to address some Christmas cards, deciding who's in and who's out on this year's list. This dilemma has never been better expressed than by the Nova Scotia writer Ernest Buckler. When I was the host of

➤ *THE TWIN TOWERS OF TORONTO'S CITY HALL FORM THE BACKDROP FOR LATE-NIGHT SKATERS ON THE RINK AT NATHAN PHILLIPS SQUARE. FOR TWO MONTHS EACH YEAR CANADA'S LARGEST CITY IS A FAIRYLAND OF CHRISTMAS LIGHTS*

Morningside, I had the pleasure of visiting him in his rural Nova Scotia home. Buckler was a bachelor who lived alone, in the neatest, cleanest little house I ever saw. He had a very real, very vibrant girlfriend who lived not far away.

After interviewing Buckler about his classic books, *The Mountain and the Valley* and *Ox Bells and Fireflies,* my next assignment was to read one of his stories to him. I read by the natural light of the setting sun, which diminished as I got into the story. I had neglected to bring my reading glasses, so it was

a race between the sun and me to see who would finish first. The story was about a man's dying moments on this earth, and the situation of the dying light of the sunset gave a particular desperation and poignancy to my voice that suited the situation.

Here is Ernest Buckler in another mood. Although mostly known for more serious writing, he did publish a delightful book of comic essays and poems called *Whirligig.* One of them deals with the annual dilemma of sending Christmas cards: "It's Not the Thought, It's the Card," by Ernest Buckler.

PART 14

Do hope you
are well?

BY ERNEST BUCKLER

LET'S FACE IT — THE CHIEF CONCERN IN THE matter of Christmas cards is to hit on a parity as exact as possible between the one you send and the one you get. What bugs you more than to send Al and Gertie a twenty-cent card, sealed, with a long chatty note (outlining among other things your dreadful siege with a ruptured disc), and get back a sleazy nickel job, unsealed, and bearing the casual scrawl, "Do hope you are well"? My wife and I have taken a hard-headed look at this problem and I feel like passing along the scientific method we came up with, for what it's worth.

Last year we rated each card, as received, on a point basis. Feature by feature. Our ratings may not be yours, of course; but just by way of illustration these are some of the main assessments we worked out.

Card itself. Allot it exactly as many points as it cost in cents. At first you may have trouble gauging the price of those odd specimens which feature one of Picasso's two-headed guitar players or a profile of the Australian heath hen, but with a little practise and research you'd be surprised how soon you get their number too. (What such cards have to do with Christmas, *any*way, is something that doesn't concern us here.)

Envelope. Score this as follows. Sealed, score 8. Unsealed, score 6.

Notes included. These would seem to present an insuperable problem. But it's quite simple. There are basically only two kinds of note. One a really warm, friendly, bringing-up-to-date type. The other, a plain between-the-lines boast of how the sender's status symbols have mushroomed during the past year. Score the first type plus 15, the latter minus 15. The inscription, "Writing later," which will turn out almost invariably to have been an outright lie, and brazenly perpetrated as such merely to let the sender off writing anything now, should be scored minus 10.

Snapshots enclosed. Score these on precisely the same principle as the notes. To the one which shows the man with less hair left on his head than you yourself have and his wife somewhat fatter than yours (Good old Henry and Bess!), give a rating of plus 16. To the one which shows a last-summer shot of husband and wife trimly ascotted and espadrilled before the Elbow Beach Hotel in Bermuda or on the shoreline of some Aegean inlet (at which time you and your wife were battling mosquitos at Kamp Kozy, with a skunk under the verandah), give a rating of minus 16.

If this sounds impossibly complicated, it's not. You get the hang of it in no time at all. And it turns the usual drudgery of Christmas cards into a challenge, a game. Before we hit on this present system in our house we never knew where we were.

I remember one year the last item on our list was Fred and Mabel, and we had nothing but 15-cent cards left. "I'm sure they only sent us a five-cent card last year," my wife said. "And one of those kids' cards at that, that you always have left over out of a box. Well, they're not going to get one of these nice hollys!" She proceeded to run the car out and drive four miles into town for a five-center.

"But it'll cost you twice as much for gas as you'll save," I protested.

"That's not the idea," she said.

Another time, we'd written our final card, crept up to bed, and sunk into the sleep of exhaustion. Around two o'clock I was awakened to find the light on and my wife in her dressing gown headed downstairs.

"Where are you going?" I said.

"It just this minute came to me," she said. "Last year, Eunice put 'Sincerely' on their card, instead of 'Love' like she always does — and tonight here I went and wrote on ours, 'If you're down this way next summer, you must come see us.' I underlined the 'must.' I'm going down to rub out that underlining before I forget it."

"But she'll see it's been rubbed out," I said.

"I know," she said. "That's the whole point."

I think it was then I first realized that some sort of *standard* procedure must be devised, to replace this constant makeshift.

It need scarcely be said that the quirks of this business (I nearly said racket) are legion. But let one example speak for all. Our neighbor to the west shares a rural mailbox with us. Each year I place our card to him and his wife in this box, often on the very morning he's already deposited in it their card to us. The maildriver picks up both cards, totes them four miles to the post office in town. There the sweating extra help sort them, date-stamp them, and return them to the same maildriver — who totes them back that same afternoon and leaves them cheek by jowl again in the same box they started from.

Which brings me to a final reflection. On the display of cards about the house. Naturally you like to exhibit the cream of the crop in the most conspicuous spots. But don't forget these same neighbors. If they come to call, they will eye the room like hawkshaws until they've located the placement of their own. If it's definitely in eclipse, or almost totally screened by the carrot fern, well . . .

One short postscript. A friend of mine tells me that when *he* wants to prune the dead wood off his list he simply sends each discard a card, sealed, but without postage. That means, of course, that each has to pay double postage for it on the other end. Repeat this for two years running, he says, and you'll never be troubled with one of them again.

But who could be as calculating as that?

IT'S NOT THE THOUGHT, IT'S THE CARD

> *FOR AS FAR AS THE EYE CAN SEE, RANK UPON RANK OF SNOWY MOUNTAINS FILL BRITISH COLUMBIA'S LANDSCAPE; BELOW, A SLEIGH RIDE IN ALBERTA*

THOUGHTS ABOUT CHRISTMAS AWAY

I CANNOT IMAGINE ANYBODY DELIBERATELY choosing to be away from home on Christmas Day. A Boxing Day exodus to remote climes I can understand, but the day itself belongs to home and hearth. Despite this fact, many of us have found ourselves in strange places on Christmas Day.

Performers are used to working on holidays, but only a minority are busy on Christmas Day. When I did a season with the Bristol Old Vic, I was cast as the juvenile lead in an original Christmas musical called *The Merry Gentleman* (alias Father Christmas), and it opened on Christmas Day. I can't remember any details about Christmas that year except that I was required to sing two numbers in the show (one of which was called "There's Only One Father Christmas") and I can't sing on key to save my soul. So Christmas for me that year was one long nervous breakdown.

The one strange place in which I have never found myself on December 25 is Hollywood. I lived there for almost five years, and each year I saw the pale green plastic trees being strung up on Hollywood Boulevard and the sign in a department store parking lot that read "Park! The Herald Angels Sing!" Inside the store were carollers sweating in Dickensian hats and Victorian mufflers. They would be arrested by the Beverly Hills motorcycle police if they tried to stroll the streets. Christmas trees could cost up to three hundred dollars and it was extra if you wanted the branches sprayed with Styrofoam snow. I shuddered at the thought of spending a smoggy Yule with mulled wine by somebody's swimming pool. It never happened. Each time I managed to get my family back to Canada to real fir trees with real snow on them.

Except once: It was the first year I spent in the movie capital. I was under contract to Paramount Pictures, in a year when that studio made only two feature films, a Jerry Lewis picture and a Grade B horror film called *I Married a Monster from Outer Space.* I was in neither of them and spent my time being loaned out for various TV shows. In the two weeks before Christmas in 1958, I was doing a Desilu Playhouse one-hour comedy drama starring Ernie Kovacs. He was the gentle hero, I was the nasty villain. Playing a walk-on part with a couple of lines was a handsome and humorous young actor called Michael Landon, soon to be Little Joe in a new TV series with Lorne Greene called *Bonanza.* The show was fun to do and Kovacs

was a delight to work with, relaxed and generous and smoking cigars that looked to be half a metre long.

In the middle of rehearsals, my New York agent called and told me my film contract was not likely to be renewed. I actually breathed a sigh of relief, which shocked her. My film career had amounted to a well-subsidized sabbatical from theatre and I was anxious to get back. Two days later, my agent called again, very excited. John Barrymore Jr. had walked out of rehearsals of the national tour of *Look Back in Anger*, phoned the next day from Rome to say that he couldn't handle the responsibilities of the part (it's longer than the role of Hamlet) and said goodbye and good luck. The production was scheduled to open in less than a week. I would have to learn this enormous role while I finished filming the TV show, rush away on Christmas Eve, rehearse Christmas Day and Boxing Day and open the following night.

My film career was closing, but if I took the chance of a lifetime, my theatrical career would be back on track with a vengeance. I finished the TV show about six o'clock on Christmas Eve, drove home clutching a bottle of expensive champagne from the ever-generous Ernie Kovacs and kissed my teary wife and daughters goodbye, leaving them to the tropical rigours of a Hollywood Christmas. My Christmas Day was spent eating an Automat hamburger and gulping large quantities of grapefruit juice so I could stay awake to learn the rest of my lines. Opening night, just before I went on stage, I knelt down in my dressing room and prayed to God to get me through this night. I hadn't done that in a long, long time.

I N 1970 I WAS PART OF A CONCERT PARTY DOING a Christmas show in Alert, Northwest Territories, on the northern tip of Ellesmere Island. It's the northernmost settlement on the face of the earth. We were flown from the Downsview airport in Toronto to a U.S. base in Greenland in a Hercules transport aircraft whose comfort station consisted of a lone chemical bucket. We stayed overnight

> *IN A WELL-KNOWN CANADIAN RITUAL, A FATHER AND SON RETURN FROM THE WOODS WITH A TREE THEY CHOSE AND CUT. SOON THE TREE WILL BE DECKED OUT WITH SPARKLING LIGHTS, MULTI-COLOURED BALLS, HANDMADE DECORATIONS AND TINSEL, TOPPED WITH AN ANGEL OR STAR. ON CHRISTMAS EVE, GIFTS FROM FAMILY, FRIENDS AND SANTA WILL APPEAR UNDER THE TREE, AND THE YOUNG BOY WILL HAVE NEW MEMORIES TO ENJOY THROUGHOUT HIS LIFE. AT SWAN RIVER, MANITOBA, BELOW, TWO HORSES WEARING THEIR THICK WINTER COATS ARE PREPARED FOR ANOTHER PRAIRIE WINTER*

at the base, playing the slot machines and feeling as if we were in a kind of olive-drab Las Vegas. The next morning, which dawned as black as pitch (and stays that way for months), we were flown to Alert, but this time our Hercules ran into very rough turbulence. I remember one of the musicians, Lou Lewis, putting on his yarmulke and saying a prayer for all of us. It worked. We landed.

We were a mixed bag of entertainers: top CBC studio musicians; Dianne Brooks, a wonderful jazz singer; Marie-France Beaulieu, Miss Canada for that year; two acrobatic dancers with flaming batons; a magician who secreted tiny birds all over his body; and me, the master of ceremonies. Perhaps I should rephrase that, lest you are led to think that I was secreted along with the tiny birds.

When we landed in Alert, the temperature was between minus fifty and minus fifty-five degrees Celsius. Covered snowmobiles were waiting to take us to the base, but in the thirty or forty seconds we were exposed to the fierce Arctic air, I

could feel my fingers start to bend toward each other as if to huddle for warmth inside my gloves.

Alert is a base for Canadian Forces engaged in all kinds of work that nobody is allowed to know about. There was a staff of two hundred, including one female, a nurse, most of whom were there for six months. The men count time by the number of "herks," or flights, out of the base that remain before they will be up and away and out of there themselves. There were rumours that some personnel spent a lot of time in the gym in the hope that a deliberate injury would shorten the sojourn.

Although it was a few days before Christmas, the base decided it would celebrate the holiday while we were there. We played two identical shows so that the entire staff could get to see us. It was the most enthusiastic audience any of us had ever come across. But the biggest surprise was provided by the base staff after our shows. They served us an elaborate buffet that would not have looked out of place in the finest hotel. We learned later that the whole complement of the base had pooled

its Christmas rations in order to feed the special guests.

Last year, Catherine and I flew to the Canadian Forces base in Lahr, Germany, for a special pre-Christmas telethon to raise money for blind children. As part of the fund-raising, we gave a concert for the troops, some of whom were about to leave for the Persian Gulf. My most searing memory of the entire experience was sitting back stage while Catherine sang, then getting into my "drag" costume as Mrs. Valerie Rosedale. As I gathered myself together — high heels, earrings, bright red dress — I suddenly realized that one prop had been left behind in Canada: Valerie's wig. I almost had a heart seizure. Catherine was just finishing her last song; I was to go on next. Suddenly I saw a prop that I had intended to use later for my other character, Charlie Farquharson. It was a Tilley hat, the kind that had become official issue for Canadian troops in Saudi Arabia. With a swoop I grabbed it, put it on my head at a rakish angle and strode on stage, my heart still pounding, announcing that Valerie was going to the Gulf.

PART 16

MORE CHRISTMAS MEMORIES

AS AN AVID STUDENT OF CANADIAN HISTORY, I was fascinated to learn about the celebration of Christmas through the half millennium of our colonial past. I doubt if the Vikings took time out for the birth of Christ, but no doubt they burned a Yule log in Greenland, if they could find one. Perhaps that would be more likely at L'Anse aux Meadows, their briefly maintained settlement in Newfoundland, which they called Vinland.

But what about the Portuguese fishermen who fished those waters well before Christopher Columbus thought he had discovered North America (actually it was Cuba and the Dominican Republic)? Evidence seems to indicate that they were fair-weather visitors who ventured only in summer.

The first indication of a blowout feast and turkey shoot with sweet potatoes on the side was in 1604, organized at what is today Annapolis Royal, Nova Scotia, by Samuel de Champlain's buddy Pierre du Gua de Monts. Champlain established the Order of Good Cheer, which still prevails; every distinguished visitor to Nova Scotia is made an honorary member. I remember the illustration by C. W. Jefferys in my high school history book that showed a bunch of bearded gentlemen in tights and bloomers bearing huge trays of cooked food, led by a gent with a napkin over his right shoulder and holding a staff very like the type used by drum majorettes. Two musicians tootle away as the procession approaches the banquet tables. The guests are natives, smoking pipes. The date was closer to Thanksgiving than Christmas, but it was a tasty start and a tradition that is still honoured, in name at any rate.

Two years later a bunch of Breton farmers arrived to settle the place, including a young lawyer, Marc Lescarbot, who became Canada's first poet and dramatist when he composed a masque, *The Theatre of Neptune.* Neptune Theatre later moved to Halifax (much later, 1963) and long may it thrive.

The clampdown on Christmas that the Puritans brought to the shores of North America affected Canada too. Catharine Parr Traill, who roughed it in the Peterborough bush next door to her sister Susanna Moodie, wrote in her diary in 1832 that nobody seemed to take any notice of Christmas . . . "cold indifference" were her words. Church was very sparsely attended, and if Mrs. Traill hadn't dragged some wintergreen berries into the house to make a wreath, the day would have passed unobserved.

Sir John Franklin, on his second Arctic exploration expedition, in 1825, taught the native population to play a game called snapdragon, which consists of snatching raisins from a bowl of burning brandy. In 1845 Franklin disappeared in an attempt to locate the Northwest Passage, and many expeditions were launched in vain to try to find him. One of these unsuccessful ventures was trapped in Arctic ice for two winters. Christmas dinner consisted of pork and beans, and the

➤ *GRAIN ELEVATORS DOMINATE A PRAIRIE VISTA IN MANITOBA; LIKE SOMETHING FROM A CHRISTMAS STORYBOOK, A HERD OF ELK, ABOVE, GAMBOLS IN THE WOODS NEAR JASPER, ALBERTA*

eighteen-man crew shared the ship's last bottle of wine.

The first important Canadian painter-explorer, Paul Kane, had interesting Christmas fare presented to him on his trip out West in the 1840s: whitefish browned in buffalo marrow, with beaver tails, buffalo tongue and something called *mouffle*, which turned out to be dried moose nose.

Rev. John McDougall, a Methodist missionary who established a mission one hundred and forty-five kilometres northeast of Fort Edmonton, had a prairie Christmas dinner in 1864 that consisted of buffalo tongue, beaver tail, moose nose, prairie chicken and wildcat. He also had a toothache that lasted for nine years, until he could get back East to a dentist.

A young American naturalist, Robert Kennicott, was the first English-speaking scientist to visit the Yukon basin. The year was 1861 and Kennicott reached Fort Yukon after having Christmas dinner en route, consisting of whitefish boiled up with melted moose tallow. He was received by James Flett, originally from the Orkney Islands, and treated to a second Christmas dinner of "caribou steak, fat-back, tongues, bango and tea."

In Dawson, people had a simple method of Neighbourhood Watch. If there was no smoke coming from your neighbour's chimney, it was a sure sign of trouble. Somebody living next door to a former prostitute informed the town doctor that there was no smoke from her chimney on Christmas morning. The doctor reluctantly left his warm home and investigated. He discovered an empty whiskey bottle on a bedside table, and in the bed, partially uncovered, was the young woman, frozen to death.

In 1926 Edgar Christian and two companions felt lucky to have some bannock and an Arctic hare for their holiday dinner when they were wintering on the Thelon River in the Northwest Territories. All three later died of starvation.

The Dirty Thirties in Saskatchewan produced some innovative menus for Christmas

➤ *DOGSLEDS WERE OFTEN THE ONLY MEANS OF WINTER TRANSPORTATION AVAILABLE TO CANADA'S NATIVE POPULATION AND THE EARLY PIONEERS IN OUR NORTH AND WEST. TODAY, MOST TEAMS ARE MAINTAINED STRICTLY FOR SPORT AND RECREATION*

dinner. Fortunately, partridges and prairie chickens were easily available: they seemed to be monumentally stupid as they sat on frozen stooks and let themselves be shot at with a .22. The rest of Christmas dinner was usually rutabagas, potatoes, onions, and for tea . . . scorched barley.

In Victoria, British Columbia, during the 1930s, the painter Emily Carr had her own reaction to Christmas. "Praise be! It's over! Why do we do it? It is not Christian. We've turkeyed and mince-pied and exchanged gifts and kissed all round and written and received mail sacks of letters. Oh, I'd have loved to sneak off to the woods and be hidden, the week before and the week behind Christmas, and remember the real meaning of it and give thanks in my heart. I love my friends for their kind thoughts of me, but it's all wrong; it's cheap and commercial and fluffy. You can point to all the full churches and special music and decorations, but what does it all mean to them? The girls [her sisters Alice and Lizzie] would say shame and shame again on me. I get more rebellious every year."

Perhaps the most tragic Christmas in Canada's history was in 1941. That's when officers and men of the Winnipeg Grenadiers and the Royal Rifles of Canada had to surrender to the Japanese on Christmas afternoon in Hong Kong. Five hundred and fifty of the two thousand never returned, and of those who did, many had to be carried aboard the troopship in stretchers, and many more weighed less than forty-five kilograms.

A happier Christmas memory was the birth of Justin Trudeau on December 25, 1972, followed two years later by his brother Sasha on the same day. The hat trick was not completed by their brother, Michel, who arrived closer to Halloween.

John Macfie, the unofficial historian of Parry Sound District, was in an RCAF training flight with me in 1944. He has collected a wonderful series of interviews about old-time logging days around Parry Sound. My favourite Christmas tale was told

> *OUR FOREFATHERS WERE KNOWN TO SKI ON BARREL STAVES WITH ROPE BINDINGS, BUT THESE DAYS EVEN THE YOUNGEST DOWNHILLER PUTS HIGH-TECH GEAR AND DAY-GLO OUTFITS ON HIS OR HER CHRISTMAS WISH LIST*

to him by a man called Chris Watts about a logging camp cook named Percy Roe. I have no idea what he cooked for Christmas dinner, but Percy had feet that were size four and a half. When he went to town to buy the food for the Christmas spread, he got a little tight while there and picked up a pair of women's shoes, size four and a half. That night he waited till everybody in the lumber camp was asleep, got dressed with the brand-new pumps and walked all over camp in the freshly fallen snow. Next

morning the camp officials were furious to find that some woman had been roaming around in a place where she had no business, and all the lumberjacks were "whistlin', whinnerin'," and trying to find her.

My most vivid memories of Christmas seem to be from when times were toughest. I remember distinctly the difference between the end of the 1920s and the beginning of the 1930s, even though I was very young at the time. Suddenly there was

less under the tree, and you didn't always get what you wanted. There was one Christmas I asked for a windbreaker that had a specific pattern to it. When the day came, I got one that had no pattern and was a rather drab dark green. My parents had done their very best, and I wish now that I had realized how much they must have sacrificed to get it for me. Instead I rushed up to my room and sulked for hours. That's my most vibrant Christmas memory and I wish to heaven I could undo it.

PART 17

THE NIGHT BEFORE CHRISTMAS IN NEWFOUNDLAND

BY BOB YOUDEN

T WAS D'NIGHT AFORE CHRISTMAS
Down 'ere in Newfoundland
An' dere was h'ice an' big snowdrifts
A plenty on 'and.
Wit' d'kids
All a sleepin'

H'up stairs
In d'loft
An' Mudder in d'kitchen — Cookin' h'up
a big scoff.
Den I was cuttin' some
Splits fer d'stove
An' Mudder was bakin' some bread —
Jus' four loaves
Wit' peas puddin' an' cabbage
Some spuds an' carn beef
Jus' tinkin' about it

Sure t'will be a fine feast.
Den down be d'warf
Dere arose some
big clatter,
I t'ought dat
Garge Murphy
fell h'off
d'flake ladder.
I runs to d'door
Like d'clap of a bell
Caught me toe

But
dere was a punt
Pulled by eight
hardy moose.
And a fat
little skipper
Wit a h'oar
in 'ee's 'and . . .
Get up dere
Mulrooney
To d'top of d'ill

in the rug . . .
An' be jumpins'
I fell.
H'as I gawked in d'garden
And h'out on d'bay
B'y d'cat got me tongue
I 'ad nuttin' t'say.
I t'ought t'meself
Screech is alright.
But a little too much
Will muck up
yer sight.
H'as me h'eyes came
accustomed to
D'wind h'an d'snow
Is dis what 'tis like
When yer mind starts t'go?
I t'ought fer d'minit
Dat me noggin' come loose
But dere was a punt
Pulled by eight hardy moose.
An' a fat little skipper
Wit a h'oar in 'ee's 'and
'Ee was scullin' d'punt
From d' h'ice to d'land
Den h'up tru d'garden
D'punt, she fair came.
An' I 'eard d'red skipper
Call each moose by name
Now move along Brian
an' John an' Bill.
Get up dere Mulrooney
To d'top of d'ill
And den 'ee 'ollered
to d'ones in d'front
Now Jerry an' Neil
Keep pullin' dis punt!
To d'top of d'shed
An' den h'onto d'roofs
You could tell dey was h'up dere
By d'sound of d'oofs.
Den h'over d'loft

Dere rose such a clatter
An' I t'ought what
might happen h'if
Dem moose was much
fatter!
I was feared fer a second
D'shingles might peel
From d'scrapin' an'
scratchin' of d'big punt's keel
Den down tru d'chimney
D' h'ole skipper 'ee came . . .
An' of course
It was Santa —
To use 'ee's right name.
Den h'out in
D'front room
A black cloud arose
D'soot looked like spume
From a whale
When she blows.
'Ee stood fer a minit
To Size h'up d'place
Wit black soot an' h'ashes
All h'over 'ee's face.
I t'ought to meself
H'as I gawked at d'man
What fine sealskin mittens
'Ee 'ad on ee's 'ands.
An' glossy new gumboots
To cover 'ee's feet
I couldn't imagine
'Ow 'ee kept 'em so neat.
'Ee 'ad a sou'wester who's color was red
An' dis 'ee 'ad perched on d'back of 'ee's 'ead
Wit' dem fine red h'oil skins like I never saw afore
Dat fitted too tight an' reached down to d'floor.
'Ee's face it was worn
An' weathered an' wrinkled
But 'ee's sparklin' blue h'eyes'
Still 'eld to der twinkle.
An' now when I looked
I saw naught but 'ee's back

H'as 'ee wrestled and juggled
D'gifts in 'ee's sack.
Den to d'mantle h'as 'ee lifted d'sox
H'apples an' h'ranges an' small toys in a box.
'Ee topped h'off each one
Fer d'garls h'an' d'b'ys
Wit' a small bag of bulls eyes
an' small wooden toys.
'Ee looked so 'appy an' jolly an' fine
H'as 'ee took a great gulp of dogberry wine.
'Ee tasted d'fruit cake and den figgy duff
Den 'ee spoke to 'eeself'
"Dis sure is fine stuff!"
'Ee tied h'up d'sack
Wit' a big granny knot
Den rested 'ee's 'ands
On d'top of 'ee's pot.
Now to d'chimney
Ee went wit a dash,
H'as ee's h'eyes crossed d'room
Wit' a flicker an' flash,
Now sure I must say
Dat 'ee cut a fine figger.
H'as 'ee slipped h'up d'chimney
Like a bright squid jigger
'Ee walked cross d'roof
Back to d'front.
An' I feared 'ee might slip
H'as 'ee got in d'punt.
D'house gave a shake
From d'roof to d'floor
H'as Santa took charge
Of d'big scullin' h'oar.
Den down tru d'garden
An' h'onto d'bay
Midst d'clammer of 'oofs
I 'eard 'im say:
'Tis another year gone
God Bless you an' yours
May 'ee grant you . . .
FAIR WINDS
As you bend at d'oars.

PART 18

CHRISTMAS IN PRINCE EDWARD ISLAND

THE CANADIAN CHRISTMAS QUILT

IN THE DEAD OF WINTER IN 1966 SOME OF US FROM *Singalong Jubilee* went to Prince Edward Island to perform at Confederation Centre. It was my first trip to the island and the crossing was so rough we had to strap the musical instruments to the railings of the ferry. The boat lunged up and down, breaking the ice in the strait. The gale-force winds and heavy snow didn't help to make a good impression on my maiden voyage. The show went well, however, and the islanders were warm and friendly people, just the opposite of the long bleak days they endure in the winter.

Some months later I was asked by Jack MacAndrew, who ran Confederation Centre at the time, to come and open the cabaret after the theatre. I turned him down flat, saying I had no desire to ever return to Prince Edward Island. After many phone calls and assurances from this native islander that it was quite beautiful in summer, I finally gave in. And I was astounded by the transformation of this small slip of land in the Gulf of St. Lawrence. The rolling hills with their different hues of green reminded me of the paddocks in Ireland. The rich red clay along the two-lane highways, bordered by mauve and pink lupins, was such a picture. The miles and miles of pale dunes, the fabulous beaches, the blackness of the night sky, with more stars than I have ever seen anywhere in the world, the fresh fish and lobster — all of this convinced me that it was indeed different in summer. I got the island bug.

After that first summer I returned many times to Prince Edward Island, sometimes for work, sometimes just to get what I call my "island fix." Then, a number of years ago, Donald and I were doing a revue for the festival and I requested accommodation outside of Charlottetown. They thought I was mad, wanting to drive the half hour to the theatre every night (tell that to a cottager in Upper Canada). We rented a gem of a place overlooking the water, a Cape Cod cottage filled with wonderful pine. I adored it. Using a little psychology, I let Donald decide we should buy it, and now we look forward to

➤ FISHING BOATS WAIT OUT THE WINTER IN NORTH RUSTICO, PRINCE EDWARD ISLAND. WE LOVE THE PEOPLE ON THE ISLAND, THEIR KINDNESS, THEIR SENSE OF FUN AND THEIR QUALITY OF LIFE

our short stay every summer. The lobster beds are out our front door, the lobster pound is just up the hill and great blue herons take off from our dock. But most of all, I love the people in the village. I love their kindness, their sense of fun and their quality of life. Over the years we've made wonderful friends.

If you come from the island you are usually a Mc or a Mac, and if you're not then you're a Gallant or an Arsenault. Tommy Gallant lives just at the top of the hill with his wife, Anita, and until about two years ago, Tommy was a fisherman. He has a sweet, gentle manner and he loves to tell stories, and no matter how many times you've heard them, you love to hear them again. Here's Tommy talking about Christmas on the island:

"I want to tell you about my father, Comin' Handy Christmas, who was a fisherman by trade. He decided he'd make a little mash and get ready for Christmas, and so he did. So my mother approached him Christmas Eve to go out and get a chicken or a rooster for Christmas Day. So he went up to the neighbour's and he got a — the neighbour was Arthur Simpson, right near by — and he asked him if he could get an old hen or something for Christmas dinner. Arthur said, 'Henry, if you can catch one of those old chickens, you can have it.' So he spotted an old rooster and he grabbed 'im and he lugged 'im home. He cut the head off the thing and he picked it and all, and he took it to the house. So his mash was brewin' away and he stayed at it pretty well Christmas Eve. Christmas mornin' come along and my mother took the chicken and she boiled and she boiled and she boiled. It was pretty thin and bony, so she roasted it. And there was a bunch of us kids — ten boys and two girls — and dinner was started to get ready. When everything was put on the table, my father at this time was pretty well tanked. He sat at the end of the table and of course he took the old butcher knife and he thought he should carve the chicken. And all of us started to sing out, 'Give me a leg, Pop! A leg, Pop! A leg, Pop!' He said what in the hell you think I got here, a spider?

"Another year my father was put in jail for six months. It was during the winter, so Christmas come up, and the neighbour, Arthur Simpson, had to act as Santa Claus. So my oldest brother, Reggie, come down Christmas Eve and he was sitting around and Arthur said you better go to bed, Reggie, 'cause this is Christmas Eve and you may get a horse tomorrow mornin' in your stockin'. Anyway, the next mornin' he gets up, bright and early, and by gosh he looked in his stocking and there was a brown paper bag, and he seen there was something in it. He pulled it out and it was all horse dung, the bag was full, and he was quite put out, quite cross about it. The neighbour come down later and said, 'Well, Reggie, did you get something from Santa Claus?' He said, 'I got this horse poop!' Arthur said, 'By God, Reggie, you shoulda got up a little earlier, you coulda got the horse!'

"My father, one winter he had twelve hens and a little old henhouse. Pretty cold winter, terrible cold. The farmers used to come through our yard in the winter, the road went through our

yard. And they used to come into our house to get warm. And this morning a farmer come into our house and my father was sittin' by the stove with a big sheepskin coat on. And the farmer said, 'Awful cold mornin', Henry.' 'Yes,' my father said, 'it's chilly and frosty, but it's not cold.' And of course him sittin' by the stove, big fire on and a big sheepskin coat on. So the farmer says to him, 'You have some hens, Henry.' 'Yes,' he said, 'I have twelve hens.' And the farmer says, 'Are they layin'?' And he said, 'Yes, twelve of them are layin'.' And the farmer says, 'You don't tell me. Twelve of them are layin'?' 'Yes,' he said, 'they are.' And the farmer says, 'When I come through your yard, I could see right through the henhouse.' 'Yes,' he said, 'but I didn't tell you how they're layin'. They froze to death, all of them, last night. They're layin' dead.'"

The Mennonites at Christmas

DONALD AND I WERE CURIOUS ABOUT THE MENNONITES'
Christmas traditions, but we didn't know any Mennonites on a personal basis. We always speak with them when we're shopping at the Saturday market near Kitchener-Waterloo, Ontario, and the Mennonites we deal with seem very jolly and pleasant, but we never get beyond the role of customer. Finally, though, a friend introduced us to someone who could help.

Peter Etril Snyder is from a Mennonite family and is a prodigious painter, recently commissioned by National Trust to paint a huge mural for the company's boardroom depicting life in Canada from coast to coast. (Peter has had more commissions than the Mulroney government.) Many of his

paintings are of Mennonite country life — haying, threshing, barn raisings, logging, maple syrup making, quilting, church meetings, skating, baseball and so on.

We wondered what Peter's fellow Mennonites thought about his depictions of them. "They think people are crazy to pay me for something that shows them doing the same ordinary things they do every day of their lives." But there are no objections from the community to his paintings, which Peter paints from photographs he has taken. Although Mennonites frown on being photographed, believing that an image on paper brings unwanted attention and puffs up an individual's self-importance, the presence of his camera generally doesn't bother them. "That's because I'm one of them," he told us. "They trust me when I say that no one but me will ever look at these snapshots." Besides, most of his paintings depict group activities and rarely single out an individual.

Peter and his wife, Marilyn, who is from the same background, looked a bit perplexed when we asked them how Mennonites celebrate Christmas. "They don't really make a celebration of Christmas," they told us. "They don't exchange gifts, except within the family, and those gifts must be literally homemade. The father may make his son a sled, or the mother might sew some doll clothes for her daughter."

No Christmas trees are brought inside the houses of the Mennonite community, nor is there a candlelight service at Christmas: "No way," said Peter, "not even the coal-oil lamps used in houses." Church services at the meeting house are always held during daylight hours. Everyone is up at five o'clock for chores and by ten o'clock they are all seated for the service, which goes on until about half past twelve. The music comprises German hymns from the late seventeenth century, sung in unison without any musical accompaniment.

Canada's first Christmas tree was erected on December 24, 1781, in Sorel, Quebec, north of Montreal, by Baron Friedrich von Riedesel

There is one manner in which the Mennonites celebrate Christ's birth as a special occasion and that is with food. Christmas dinner is served at about half past one at the grandmother's house, and a large extended family gathers for the feast. There are so many people that, as on a cruise ship, there has to be more than one sitting. The men and boys are served first. The main course is either duck or goose; Mennonites don't keep turkeys because they consider them to be bad tempered. The fowl is served with mounds of mashed potatoes with lots of gravy and all kinds of home-grown vegetables. (In addition to this main meal, a cold spread of sausages and pickles and different breads is served just after three o'clock because everybody has to be back in the barn for chores at five.)

But at the main meal almost everybody is really waiting for dessert, because that is the special Christmas treat. First, mince pie with whipped cream fresh from the cow barn (Mennonites love ice cream as much as anybody, but they consider it a summertime dish). And then comes a wealth of cookies, not too rich or too sweet, but extra fancy for the special day with all kinds of sprinkles and crinkles and those little silver balls that look like ammunition for a BB gun. After dinner come extra little treats: nuts and popcorn and homemade candy. Even store-bought candy is allowed at Christmas, and there is also

homemade chocolate. Marilyn remembers with delight her mother making hand-dipped coconut balls done in pastel colours. She also remembers winning a prize for memorizing the most Bible verses; the prize was a pound of chocolate.

There is no visit from Santa Claus for Mennonite children. Their elders know the time will come when children will question the existence of such a being. If they question his existence, the elders reason, they may start to question the existence of the Creator.

NEWFOUNDLAND CHRISTMAS

JUST UP THE ROAD FROM OUR COUNTRY HOUSE ON THE way into Barrie (I call our place "Barrie Sound") is a Newfoundland fish and chip restaurant. It's run by a friendly fellow named Mitch, who works days at nearby Canadian Forces Base Borden and runs the restaurant at night, and by his wife, who runs it in the daytime and works at Barrie's Victoria Hospital at night. They're a hard-working couple.

We go there for codfish cakes and cod cheeks and cod tongues, for toutons and doughboys and fish'n brews. The pea soup and the apple crisp are good, too. Toutons (pronounced *tout'uns*, as in racetrack) are like deep-fried pancakes served sometimes with corn syrup, but most often with molasses. Doughboys are free-form dumplings that vary in shape, and fish'n brews look to me like one big codfish cake with a hint of bacon.

When we asked Mitch if any of those items appeared on the Christmas menu in his boyhood home in St. John's, he laughed uproariously. "Nah, we has jist what you mainlanders has . . . goose wit' bread stuffin', and a Jigg dinner folleyed by duff wit' a rum sauce." The Jigg dinner is one of Catherine's favourites: it's named after the comic strip character in *Maggie and Jiggs* who loved corned beef and cabbage. Newfoundlanders call it salt beef and at Christmas they add turnip, carrots, potatoes and sometimes roast beef. In tough times the duff (Christmas pudding) is replaced by bread and molasses or a big doughboy stuffed with raisins or canned fruit. And Newfoundlanders always have fresh-baked bread, three hundred and sixty-five days a year. Mitch said his mother baked bread twice a day, at least six loaves, and most of it ended up soaked in molasses.

Mitch told us that Newfoundland kids had a surefire way of communicating with Santa Claus. They would write him a letter and, instead of mailing it, would put it in the stove. They firmly believed that when the ashes flew up the chimney, they would go straight to the North Pole. Children on the Rock

 THE LIGHTHOUSE AT CAPE SPEAR, NEWFOUNDLAND

probably had twice as much faith in St. Nick as other kids because they hung up their stockings twice a year, on Christmas Eve and on January 5, the "old Christmas Eve." What they would find each time was very modest, an orange or an apple, maybe some grapes, hard rock candy, a bull's-eye or two and molasses kisses.

The hardest thing about Christmas when he was young, Mitch said, was trying to get to sleep on Christmas Eve. There weren't many cars in St. John's back in the late 1930s and early 1940s, but there were lots of horse-drawn sleighs. Every time young Mitch heard the sound of sleigh bells, he would jump up and run to the window. He probably fell asleep from exhaustion.

His father, an irrepressible comedian, added to the complications. One Christmas when Mitch was about four years old, his father took the double-barrelled shotgun out back of their house. They lived on the edge of St. John's next to a wooded area, and his dad would usually come back with a rabbit for the stew. But this particular Christmas Eve the family sat and waited supper for him. Then they heard the blast of a shotgun at extremely close quarters. Mitch's dad came in the back door with no rabbits and with a long sad face. "I'm sorry, kids. I didn't mean it, but I just shot Sandy Claws!"

CHRISTMAS IN TRINIDAD

ELIZABETH PAUL COMES FROM PORT OF SPAIN, Trinidad, and I feel a special kinship with her because that is the birthplace of my beloved daughter, Kelley. (I was fulfilling a singing engagement at the Trinidad Hilton in Port of Spain when Kelley arrived two months early. Have you ever had labour pains to the tune of "Yellow Bird"? Personally, I couldn't sing that song for years.)

Kelley was born in January, so I missed all the festivities of Christmas, but Elizabeth Paul has told us all about them.

Trinidad, like Canada, is a multicultural country, with very strong Spanish and French influences, along with its later British traditions. The intense preparation for Christmas, Elizabeth told us, begins at the start of December with the women doing housecleaning the way we do spring cleaning here, and I do mean *cleaning.* The mahogany floors are stripped, sanded, stained and polished, as are all the wood furnishings in the house. Elizabeth said her mother even made new mattresses for the beds, with new casings and stuffing.

Port of Spain resembles a ghost town during this time as most people are indoors, scrubbing and scouring. But even before

⋀ *A Haida totem pole braves the cold in Jasper, Alberta*

that, other pre-Christmas activities are under way: fruits such as raisins, figs and cherries are soaked in hundred-proof rum from one to three months for use in the Christmas cakes.

What are the men doing all this time? Two weeks before Christmas, said Elizabeth, they go out and *parang*. Parang, which comes from the Spanish, is the Trinidad version of carolling. It's a highly energetic, happy, uplifting music honouring the birth of Christ, usually accompanied by a guitar, or *quatro*, and *shack-shack*, which are like maracas. When the men go paranging from house to house, they are offered rum punch and coconut tarts or sweets such as *paimi* (pronounced *pay-me*), made from corn, dried and finely grated, then boiled and wrapped in fig leaves. But the men always make it home in time to go to church at midnight. Meanwhile, the women are busily preparing all the foods for the Christmas dinner. Almost all the baking is done December 24, up until church time. A pine tree is brought home, set up on the verandah and decorated simply with angel hair, lights and an angel on top.

The whole island sparkles with freshness on Christmas Day and is redolent with delicious aromas. It's as if the members of each household expect the Christ child to come to their home. Christmas dinner is served at noon and might include roast chicken or turkey; the national dish of pigeon, peas and rice; with side dishes of boiled sweet potatoes, dasheen (a bluish root vegetable) and plantain, a starchy vegetable that looks very

similar to bananas. Apples and grapes are special fruits served only at Christmas, but there is no real formal dessert course after the entrées because everyone is so full. Dessert is more like a snack, to be eaten later on. How sensible.

The father of the family hands out the Christmas gifts, and there is usually just one for each child. For the less fortunate children who don't receive presents, there is no teasing or one-upmanship. Instead, the presents, usually toys, are shared. There is a euphoric feeling of happiness and a real sense of community. Even if you're not talking to a neighbour for one reason or another, all is forgotten during this two-week festive time. It's one big party, and you're welcome in everyone's home.

On visits you might be served a red drink called sorrel, made from the sorrel herb; homemade ginger beer, very sharp and bitter; or traditional Trinidadian eggnog with rum, called punch cream. The latter's name may illustrate the feeling you get when you drink it and the feeling you get the morning after.

HRISTMAS IN THE PHILIPPINES

FRED MANGALLON HAS WORKED AT TORONTO'S Providence Centre, where my mother spent the last year of her life, for almost twenty years. One day during an ice cream break (I was a daily visitor back then), I asked Fred about Christmas back home in the Philippines when he was a boy.

Fred is from a large family of three boys and five girls. In his family, he told me, they put up the tree and start hanging decorations on December 15. They use egg shells, as well as tiny wrapped boxes and small plastic animals, and put a concoction made from boiled laundry soap shavings on the tree to simulate snow. The Mangallons also put a star-shaped lantern and lots of well-arranged Christmas lights in the window. The lantern is an important part of the family's traditions, for it reminds them of the star that guided the three wise men to Bethlehem.

December 15 is also the start of a ten-day period of devotion for the largely Roman Catholic population of the Philippines, with daily masses at midnight. Children can be seen on street corners singing Christmas carols in both English and Tagalog, a Filipino language. They make their own maracas using coconut shells and stones.

Christmas Day is a very special, solemn holiday, a time for prayers and the gathering of friends and loved ones. Dressed in their best clothes, youngsters go from house to house to pay their respects to their elders. They show respect by placing the backs of their hands to the forehead of the adult.

Rich or poor, you will have smoke rising from your backyard. With temperatures of about thirty degrees Celsius at that time of year, all of the cooking is done outside. The main course might be a roast suckling pig, cooked slowly for half a day, until it's tender inside and dark and crispy outside, or a stuffed chicken, a special dish served only once or twice a year. The bird is carefully boned and stuffed with ground meat, usually beef or pork, mixed with pepper, onion and garlic, then reassembled to act as the centrepiece for the table. Thin transparent noodles are cooked until they plump up and are placed on a platter in the form of a nest. The chicken is placed in the middle and garnished with green leaves and hard-boiled eggs.

A LEBANESE CHRISTMAS

OUR FRIENDS LARRY AND JEAN RASHID ARE MARONITE Christians from Lebanon who invite us to their home each year for a delicious Lebanese meal. Jean says that Easter, rather than Christmas, is the big event for Maronite Christians, but that the same dishes are served on both occasions. This usually includes a turkey or chicken, with a stuffing made from rice, pine nuts and ground lamb, and a baked dish called *kibbi*, made with cracked wheat, grated onion and ground lamb. All the ingredients for the kibbi are put through a grinder or food processor and then softened with cold water. A stuffing for the kibbi is made of pine nuts, finely chopped onion, cinnamon, allspice and more ground lamb. The kibbi goes on the bottom, the stuffing in the middle and more kibbi goes on top.

NESTOR PISTOR'S UKRAINIAN CHRISTMAS

DONALD AND I HAVE THIS WONDERFUL FRIEND IN Edmonton named Don Ast. He plays a comic character called Nestor Pistor and he is — I mean *both* of them are — Ukrainian. They are sort of interchangeable, like Don Harron and Charlie Farquharson. Here's Don (Ast, that is), or Nestor Pistor, on the Ten Days after Christmas:

"On the first day after Chrismuss my sweetie sant to me: one used Chrismuss tree.

"On the second day after Chrismuss dot gurlfriend sant to me: two purple necktie and a big used Chrismuss tree.

"On thord day frum Chrismuss mine baby sant to me: three packages ciggy papers, two purple necktie and a big used Chrismuss tree.

"On fort day frum Chrismuss that sweetgal sant to me: four pounds chewed tobacco, three package ciggy papers, two purple tie and dot used-up Chrismuss tree.

"On fift day frum Chrismuss my dolly sant to me: five golden shirt (vit ringaround caller), four pounds chewed tobacco, three package ciggy papers, two poorple tie and second-hand Chrismuss tree.

"On saxth day past Chrismuss my honya sant to me: fool-culler illstration sax book, five golden shirts, four pounds chewtobacca, three packidge ciggypaper, two poorpull tie and that same use-up Chrismuss tree.

"On savinth day off Chrismuss lite frum my life sant to me: savin burnout litebulb (don't worry they wuz frum my darkroom), sax-illstrated book, five golden shirt, four pound tobacca, three packidge cig paper, two purpill tie and a re-cycle Chrismuss tree.

"On ate day pass Chrismuss my sweety gave to me: eight cans deeo-door-ant (is dot sweety or sweaty?), seven burnup litebulb, high-culler sax book, five golden short, four chewd tobacca, three books ciggy papers, two purp tye and slitely use Chrismuss tree.

"Nine days outa Chrismuss dis gorjuss girl sands to me: nine-speed bicycle (one gear short . . . must be from Wankoover), eight can dee-ode-runt, seven washup lite bulb, sax illustrated, five golden shurt, four pound chewbacca, three books cigpaper, two poor pullnecktie and a Chrismuss fir used to be tree.

"On tanth day frum Chrismuss, dot crazy broad sant to me: tan headake tablit . . . (song driving me crazy, I gotta go lie down)."

CHRISTMAS ON BAFFIN ISLAND

FRED AND OOLANI KOMAN (HE'S UKRAINIAN, SHE'S Inuit) have been friends of ours from the time Donald was the host of *Morningside*. They live in Iqaluit, Northwest Territories, formerly known as Frobisher Bay. At Christmastime on Baffin Island there is perhaps one hour of daylight in the twenty-four, and it's more like dusk than daylight. But there's lots to do, including dancing at the church hall, where refreshments such as caribou, *muktuk* (seal blubber) and bannock are served. Bannock, a type of Arctic bread, is served every time you walk into someone's home. But the big delicacy is rotten walrus, which tastes something like very old cheese.

CROSS-COUNTRY SKIING AT LAKE LOUISE, ALBERTA

PART 19

SOMEDAY:

T HE SNOW IS GETTING HARDER AND HARDER TO SHOVEL. I'M ONLY

26 but anyone would get winded working on that heavy, wet stuff God seems to have

invented as a way of torturing people with driveways.

The irony is that it isn't even my driveway; it belongs to Barb, my sometimes girl

friend. I say sometimes because our relationship is kind of unique — sometimes we love

each other, the rest of the time we fight horrendously. Sort of like a cross between

D-Day and a cheap motel.

One of the things we disagree about most is the way she has of making me do things

around her house. So here I stoop, flinging snow and forcibly singing Christmas carols,

A CHRISTMAS STORY

'tis the season to be jolly and all that sort of stuff.

To be honest, I don't really put up much of a fight over chores like this because Barb

lives with her mother, and Anne is a wonderful old woman with a perpetually full pot of

tea. Barb's brother died a while back in a car accident, and she lost her father years

ago to cancer.

So all that's left of the family is the two of them in that old house down by the lake.

At least that's what you'd think. The truth is, for as long as I can remember, the family

has had a secret. Not a terrible secret, mind you, but a painful one nonetheless.

BY DREW HAYDEN TAYLOR

It seems that Barb and her brother weren't Anne's only children. Before they came along, she had a little girl she named Mary. The problem was that nobody outside the village knew she and Frank were married. He was in the army at the time and there was a rumour that Indians who enlisted had to give up their Indian status. Frank was able to disguise who he was, and secretly sent his pay home while he was stationed overseas.

This left Anne to raise her daughter alone, and it wasn't long before the Children's Aid Society got wind of it. To protect her husband's secret, Anne claimed the father was long gone. But the authorities took a dim view of single parents on the reserve, and they had two ways of handling the situation: ship the kids off to residential schools (which they often did even if both parents were around) or, if the children were younger, send them to foster homes.

Little Mary was taken away just before her first Christmas. The village rallied around Anne but back then native people could do little more than suffer in silence.

Time passed, Frank came home, and in a few years Barb and her brother were born. Perhaps she was making up for her lost child, but Anne spoiled them both rotten, and Barb loved it. That's why I shovel their driveway.

To the rest of the family Mary seemed like little more than a distant memory. Even Anne didn't talk about her much, although every once in a while, when she was at the pow wow or cooking a big meal for all her nephews, nieces and cousins, she would wonder aloud how she was doing. She always seemed confident that she would see her again, but most of the family tried to discourage her from this kind of talk, as though it were pointless to open up old wounds.

Every so often she'd talk to me about her Mary. It was sad but I guess she liked being sad.

"Someday she'll come home. There'll be a day when my little Mary will be standing in front of me, and I'll give her such a hug. Someday."

She always said it in a wistful sort of way, her sadness tinged with hope. I felt sorry for her, but I also admired her spirit, her belief that even after 35 years she would see her daughter again. I have trouble waiting for a pizza.

Unlike many cultures, the native community respects and honours its older people — living all those years gives them wisdom and knowledge. Anne was no different; when it came

Little

Mary was taken

away just before her

first Christmas.

The village rallied

around Anne but

native people could

do little more than

suffer in silence

to Mary, she simply knew she'd see her again.

It was about a week ago the call came. Vanessa, the receptionist at the band office, took it and then phoned to tell Anne. But Barb answered.

"Barb, I just got off the phone with some woman from Toronto."

"Thank you for phoning me up and telling me that." Barb could have a sharp tongue.

"No, you don't understand. She was looking for some information, some old information."

"Why are you bothering me? Should I care about all this?"

"Barb, listen. She wants information from about 35 years ago. She wanted to know if there have been any children given up for adoption way back then. She says she wants to find her family."

I couldn't hear what was going on, but by the sudden change in Barb's expression, I knew it was something heavy. Her eyes darted toward the living room where Anne was watching television. She seemed to study her mother, then quickly scribbled down something on a piece of paper. Her hand was shaking.

Then she hung up and joined me at the kitchen table, forgetting her coffee by the phone. She looked funny, sort of apprehensive, a bit scared. She told me about the call and I couldn't help glancing over at Anne, too.

"You should tell her."

Barb shook her head. "Why? It might not be her. Why get Mom all excited."

"Thirty-five years ago. A woman. Come on, Barb. I think you should tell her. And you know Vanessa — half the village will know by dark."

I'd never seen Barb so indecisive. If it were anything less serious, I would've teased her about it. Finally she looked back at her mother, got up and headed toward her, seeming to psych herself as she went.

I debated whether to leave. This was one of those very private family moments that I really didn't want to see. In the end, I stayed. Maybe I could be of some help.

Barb knelt in front of Anne, talking directly into her face. I couldn't hear them, the television was too loud (one of Anne's favourite soap operas, something about Mike sleeping with Mitch's old girl friend who was into drug smuggling with the father of Mike's step sister, I think). But even from the kitchen I could see Anne's eyes widen, and then go to the window.

CANADIAN • 84 • CHRISTMAS

Barb made me make all the necessary calls. She was too scared, and Anne was incapable of dialling the numbers. The piece of paper Barb gave me had a number in the city and a name, not Mary's. I listened as the phone rang all those miles away. I half-wished nobody would pick it up, but you don't always get what you want, even at Christmas.

"Good afternoon. Bain, Williams and Barnes. Can I help you?"

Lawyers. It figured. Everybody on the outside does everything through lawyers. "Yes, could I talk to Janice Wirth, please?" I put my hand over the phone. "This must be her lawyer."

"One moment please," and then I heard the familiar beeping of being put on hold. My eyes moved back and forth between Barb's nervousness and Anne's pleading curiosity. Then a new voice came on the line.

"Janice Wirth."

"Ah, yes. I believe you called the Otter Lake Reserve earlier today. I'm calling on behalf of the family you were enquiring about."

There was a slight pause. "This family had a baby girl 35 years ago?"

Her voice had the same professional tone that many of my teachers at college use. No nonsense, tell me what I want to know or I don't have any time for you. Yet in a way it was hesitant.

"That's correct," I said.

"And what was this girl's name?"

"It was Mary."

"Oh, my god!" Somewhat of a strong reaction for a lawyer. "Are you part of the family?"

"No, just a friend . . . Um, they're very anxious to meet Mary, her mother especially. What exactly is the procedure for this type of thing?"

"How many are there in the family? The mother's still alive; is the father? What about brothers and sisters?" She was becoming more and more excited.

"Wouldn't it be better if Mary talked with the family about all this?" I asked. "It's between them and her, I believe."

Another pause, and then:

"I am Mary."

Now it was my turn to pause. Anne and Barb could tell something had thrown me off. They huddled closer to me as their eyes asked questions.

"But your name's Janice Wirth," I sputtered.

Her voice started to lose its excitement and take on the professional tone again. "When I was

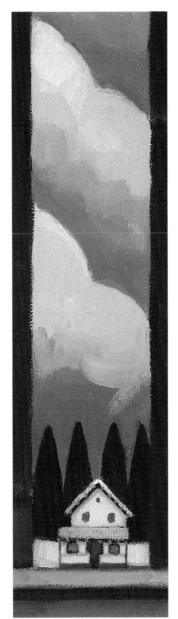

adopted, my new parents christened me Janice after a grandmother. It's only recently I discovered my birth name was Mary."

I took this all in, and tried to figure out the best way to explain it to Barb and Anne. I covered the receiver and looked at Anne. "I'm talking to Mary." How I said it so matter-of-factly I don't know.

Anne stared at me for a moment, then the tears came. She grabbed Barb and gave her as fierce a bear hug as her 100-pound body would allow. It had been a while since I'd seen her that happy.

Barb was in a daze, so I asked Anne if she wanted to talk to Mary, or Janice or what ever they decided to call her. But she shook her head — she wasn't ready — and backed away from the phone like it was red hot. "I don't want to meet her over the phone. Tell her to come here, come home as soon as possible."

Again I was left to make all the plans. Christmas was the following Tuesday but Janice agreed to drive out to the reserve on the weekend.

Anne's expression was calm, except for her eyes — they sparkled. "This is the most wonderful Christmas present I could ever ask for," she said, looking up: "Thank you, Lord. My baby's coming home."

Then she looked at me again. "I told you some day my baby would come home." Her voice had that familiar ring of wistfulness and hope, but now the sadness was gone.

The next couple of days were spent in feverish anticipation. Anne cleaned her house, and then cleaned it again until it gleamed. This was no mean feat for the old place. It's over 90 years old and constantly being renovated but nothing can hide the fact that it has a decided lean to the left (Barb calls it the "Communist house"). The band offered to build Anne a new place but she declined. "I was born in this house, and I'll die in this house." But she did agree to indoor plumbing. "Sixty years of going to the outhouse in January is enough for any sane woman." The outhouse is still out back, almost lost in the bushes.

Amid the aroma of Windex and Mop 'n Glo, Anne talked nonstop about Mary's visit. She had the whole weekend planned out — as though she could pack 35 lost years into two days. Out came the old pictures of Frank and the one photo she had of Mary as a baby. It was her pride and joy.

And as the time grew nearer, Barb too began to show some enthusiasm. The day before she even went out and chopped down a Christmas tree, which Anne said Mary could help them put up. "She'll be a real part of the family then."

Not that Barb shared all her mother's confidence. "I'm worried about Mom," she said as I helped her take the tree off the car. Anne was still puttering around inside looking for non-existent dirt to clean up. "What if Mary isn't what she expects? What if Mary doesn't like us?"

I tried to reassure her but the doubts persisted. "I've even gotten religious this Christmas. I've been praying that this whole thing goes right. I can handle it, if Mary turns out to be a bitch or something, but Mom . . . What do you think will happen?"

I shrugged. It was a big tree, hard to handle. "Don't worry about it. It's Christmas, remember — you're supposed to be jolly. Your mom's strong. And Mary spent months trying to find you two. It obviously is very important to her.

"Everything will be fine. Tomorrow you two will be the best of friends, long-lost sisters. It'll make a great movie of the week."

She laughed and shoved the tree into my ribs. We dumped it on the driveway. I'd bring it in later for the newly reformed family to decorate.

Tomorrow finally came. I was invited to be there for Mary's arrival even though I didn't really want to intrude. This was family business, personal business. Besides, *How the Grinch Stole Christmas* was on television.

The atmosphere in the now-pristine kitchen was tight. Fingers drummed on tables, tea was being consumed in massive quantities, so toilets were being flushed a lot, and heads were constantly swivelling toward the window overlooking the driveway.

Finally, we heard a car come up, and we all looked at one another, not sure how to react. Anne got up and looked out the window. She stood there for a moment, silhouetted against the winter glare. Barb and I joined her.

It was a Saab, a car Janice Wirth would drive, not Mary. It was beautiful and seemed to clash with the dirt driveway as it crept forward almost as though afraid of bumping into the frail, little house.

There's a certain knack to driving on country roads in the wintertime, and this woman just didn't have that knack. Twenty feet from the

She stood

gazing at the

house with no

discernible

expression on

her face, except

perhaps curiosity.

She was drinking

everything in

house, the Saab lost traction as she tried to manoeuvre around the Christmas tree, and plowed into the snowbank. Evidently all my shovelling had done little good.

For a few moments, nothing happened. No one got out of the car and we couldn't see in. Finally, the door opened and she appeared.

At first she seemed to be a white blur, then I realized it was the fur coat she was wearing. It seemed to rise and ebb in the wind coming off the lake, as though it were still alive. Evidently, Mary-Janice was doing very well for herself. She stood gazing at the house with no discernible expression on her face, except perhaps curiosity. She was drinking everything in, putting some pieces into the puzzle.

Anne was the first to move. She ran to the door, flung it open and stepped out on the porch. Her eyes met Mary's. No words were spoken, they just looked at each other.

Finally it dawned on me that it was 15 below out there and Anne was just wearing a blouse. Barb was staring, too. I gave her a nudge. "Mom, invite her in." She had to say it again before Anne responded, somewhat embarrassed. "I'm sorry, Mary, please come in. You must be cold."

At first Mary didn't move, then she slowly made her way to the stairs. Her shoes weren't made for walking on hard-packed snow; she almost fell twice before making it to the relative safety of the steps. She climbed slowly, getting closer and closer to Anne. It was almost like something in slow motion.

Finally they were just inches apart. Even from inside the house I could see familiar things in Mary's unfamiliar face — Anne's eyes, the little bump on Barb's nose. She wore more makeup than Barb, but the hair was the same texture.

"Baby, my baby."

Anne threw her arms around her first-born child and hugged her tightly. Mary was startled and tried to return the hug but didn't quite know how. She glanced our way and spotted Barb. It was their turn to stare at each other. Again it was Anne who broke the silence.

"Mary, this is your sister Barbara."

"My sister."

Uncharacteristically, Barb merely nodded, and just as I was wondering what the hell I was doing there, Mary noticed me. "Just a friend," I said quickly. "The guy on the phone."

Anne grabbed Mary's arm with one hand as

she wiped away some tears with the other and guided her to the kitchen table. "Welcome home. What a wonderful Christmas."

It was time for yet another cup of tea, and then the talking began. Of course, it was one-sided at first. Barb and Mary weren't willing to open up right away, but Anne talked a mile a minute and soon persuaded Mary (who had trouble responding to that name) to tell us of her search.

"It's a long story but all stories have a beginning, I guess. I always knew I was Indian, but it was just a fact of life — like being 5-foot-4 or something. Then there was Meech Lake and Elijah Harper, and then the Oka thing. Suddenly everyone at the office was asking what I thought about the situation. They wanted the 'native opinion,' but the only opinion I had was from the suburbs. I started to wonder about my past, and the more questions I was asked, the more I had questions about myself. Finally I just had to know.

"It wasn't easy. A lot of doors were slammed in my face, but I carried on. I went to the city where I grew up, found the court I was processed in and requested my adoption papers. Once I had those, I contacted the Department of Indian Affairs, presented them with the information I had, and they eventually told me what reserve I was from. Then I called here. Then you called me. And here I am."

There was an awkward silence. Then Barb asked Mary about her childhood, and she finally opened up. She described growing up in a fairly prosperous home and, unlike so many adopted native children, had no horror stories to tell. Soon everyone felt more comfortable, and Anne was fairly glowing.

The talk went on and on, punctuated only by the appearance of a fresh pot of tea. I could barely get a word in and just sat there nodding my head. But you can only nod for so long, so I finally broke into the conversation with a compliment for her Saab.

"My car! How am I gonna get it out of that snow bank? Is there a towing service nearby?"

Bingo. I couldn't have asked for a better excuse to leave them alone for a while. "You don't need a tow truck. I'll take care of it." I waved goodbye on my way out, but nobody noticed — to them I hardly existed.

The idea of shovelling more snow wasn't all that attractive, but I gritted my teeth and have

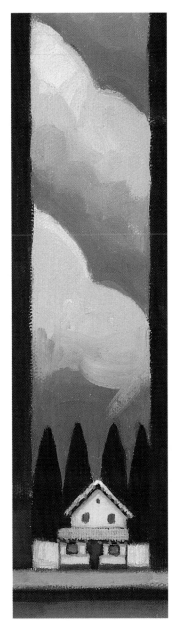

been at it for about half an hour. Every so often I see them moving about the kitchen, getting more tea, going to the bathroom. The sun has set over the lake and it's really starting to get cold, but I feel warm inside. It's Christmas, Anne has her daughter back, and Barb should be happy for a while. All is well with the world.

I've just about got the car out, and I should take the Christmas tree in pretty soon and let them do the family thing with it.

"Oh, thank you! I hoped you'd be finished by now."

Mary's enormous coat is billowing in the wind. "Oh, hi. I didn't hear you come out."

"Am I suppose to tip you or anything like that?"

Is she kidding? I just shake my head.

"Okay. Well, thank you again, and 'bye."

"You're leaving already? They have all sorts of things planned for you."

"I know, and I hate to disappoint them, but I do have other appointments to keep. I hope they won't be too upset."

I plunge my shovel into the snow and lean against the Saab, trying to figure her out. "You've given them a special Christmas. I think they want to share it with you."

"Well, sometimes you can't always get what you want."

"Mary . . ."

"Please, call me Janice."

"Janice, why did you come out here?"

"Curiosity. I had to know. I had to see. So now I know, and I've seen what I wanted to see."

She turns back toward the house, and her eyes wander from the half-hidden outhouse past the dirt driveway until they come to rest on the two figures silhouetted in the kitchen window.

I decide to push the issue. "When do you think you'll be back?"

"Oh, someday, I suppose." I recognize the tone — wistful, a bit sad but no hope.

She opens the car door and gets in. "Merry Christmas" is all she says before backing carefully out of the driveway. The last thing I see as the car disappears in the dark is the licence plate: "WIRTH." Back at the house the two figures are gone from the window.

Well, that does it. I should just call it a day, go home and see how much "egg nog" I can find.

Instead, I bend down and pick up the Christmas tree. I knew it would be a bitch getting it up those stairs.

PART 20

CATHERINE'S CHRISTMASES

SHORTLY AFTER **I** WAS BORN, MY FATHER LEFT for England and World War II. My recollections of him during those very early years are from lots of photographs and letters (he was almost a daily letter writer) and the occasional telephone call.

Our first Christmas as a family was at Canadian Forces Base Shilo in Manitoba. I was four years old. My father was a pharmacist in the Medical Corps, and we lived in a wing of the hospital. Our place was just down the hall, through the huge red fire doors, past the nurses' quarters and the operating room to my father's dispensary.

I remember that after midnight mass my parents and some of the staff were in our kitchen (where else?), digging into an enormous ham. I heard their laughter and came in to join the party. I looked under the tree and to my amazement saw three dolls: one from my parents, one from Santa and one from the nurses. I took the dolls back to the room I shared with my baby sister, Patrician Anne. What do I remember most about that first family Christmas? I wet the bed.

The next year I was asked to sing in the Christmas concert.

I was a precocious child and drove my mother crazy when my older brother went off to school and I wasn't allowed to. I don't think they had pre-school in those days, but I was so insistent that I got to go early. I loved school and my first teacher, Mrs. Read. One day I asked to be excused to go to

A FAMILY PORTRAIT IN THE HALLWAY OF OUR TORONTO HOME. THAT'S OUR DAUGHTER, KELLEY, ON THE RIGHT; THE DEBONAIR MAN ON THE LEFT IS YOU-KNOW-WHO

➤ *While we were doing research for this book, Donald and I spent several "arduous" days at the fabulous Château Lake Louise, in the Rocky Mountains west of Calgary. Here, we're learning to skate — and to stop!*

the bathroom. When I returned to the classroom, Mrs. Read asked me what I had done. I told her. She said, "And what else did you do?" I said, "I washed my hands." She asked, "What else?" I said, "Nothing." She said, "Are you sure?" I said, "Yes." Then she asked me if I had sung. I told her I didn't remember.

Apparently on the way to the loo I was singing "I've Got a Lovely Bunch of Coconuts." I had been totally unaware of it. She asked me if I would sing the song for the class. "Sure," I said, and I did. We then went to every room, from Grades 1 to 8. (I mean all of us: Mrs. Read, the whole class and me.)

Because of that incident, I was asked to sing in the Christmas school concert. My mother made me a maroon velvet dress with a lace collar, and I sang, "All I Want for Christmas Is My Two Front Teeth." It was appropriate, because I didn't have any, and my toothless picture appeared in the local newspaper.

HEN I WAS SIX, WE LIVED IN CHURCHILL, Manitoba, on Hudson Bay, just below the Arctic Circle on the 58th parallel. We had to bind two Christmas trees together to make a whole one because the north wind had blown away all the branches on one side. We had lots of guests for dinner that year, including Father Lord, the oblate priest, plus any man on the base who was alone for the holiday.

My brother, René, got an electric train . . . and it was my favourite present. I don't remember what I got, but it doesn't matter. I played with that train for hours. My mother called us to table and I was asked to say grace. I coyly refused. "Catherine Beth," my mother said, "would you please say grace?" Again I declined. She asked me again, and again the answer was "No."

I was very quietly and firmly sent to my room, without my Christmas dinner. Worse than that, I had left the train's transformer on, and when my brother tried to make it go, it was dead. So was I for the rest of that Christmas celebration. Every time I smell burning rubber, I think of that Christmas. And, by the way, I never refused to say grace again.

In 1950, with only a few days' notice, my father was whisked away to the front lines of the Korean War. Shortly after he left, we returned to my birthplace, Saint John, New Brunswick. My father wrote a letter *every day*, and he would send presents. The letters and parcels were so frequent the postman became a family friend.

We sent my father "care" packages of canned lobster, his favourite New Brunswick sardines packed in mustard, bags of dulse from the island of Grand Manan, my mother's Christmas cookies and the dark Irish fruitcake he loved, made from his mother's recipe.

He was given Christmas leave for a four-day weekend in Japan. Daddy bought and sent us beautiful gifts: a silk embroidered brown-and-yellow jacket for my brother with a dragon on the back plus a sleek remote-controlled half-metre-long speedboat; a rich emerald green silk kimono for my mother; and for my sister and me, two dolls with hand-painted faces. One had blond curls in ringlets and wore a bonnet and a pale blue dress with a three-tiered skirt; the other had dark hair and wore a black velvet bodice with a taffeta plaid skirt.

The dolls were placed under the tree, and whoever got up first was to choose the one she liked better. I was the first one up and took the blond-haired doll. I knew the really beautiful doll was meant for my sister, but I took it anyway. I still have it to this day, but it haunts me that I was so selfish. That is the most vivid memory of my seventh Christmas . . . except possibly ice skating after Christmas dinner.

When my father returned from Korea, we were posted to London, Ontario. Christmas that year meant new friends, all kinds of changes and, as always, midnight mass and wonderful food afterward. Ribbon candy, barley toys and huge bags of dulse arrived from relatives in New Brunswick.

When we moved to London, I continued to sing on children's radio shows, and I started to appear on television. TV shows were black and white and *live* in those days. I had done a number of programs, singing solos, duets and chorus work, and I felt very much at ease. But one show really stands out for me. Just before Christmas I was singing with a Roman Catholic choir. I had been given a solo in Latin, no less. When it was my turn to sing, with a big close-up of me on camera, I opened my mouth *and nothing came out.*

back to me. A beautiful blond, fair-skinned woman suddenly began singing "O Holy Night." She had a lyrical, clear soprano voice. We all applauded her, and she looked forward to singing to us every year.

In 1964 I spent my first Christmas away from home. I was to fly to Fredericton, New Brunswick, and appear in the title role in the pantomime *Cinderella*. Can you imagine what it was like to try to learn stage technique in a couple of weeks of rehearsal when I had spent most of my life on radio and television? I was not very good in the part, but the show was a great success. The big thing for me was *not* being home for Christmas. I remember calling Halifax and talking to my family and crying. Being in the newspaper every day and seeing a photograph of me in front of the theatre larger than my five-foot self . . . all this attention couldn't take the place of being home for Christmas.

In 1966 I recorded a Christmas album, and that December I was part of a group sent to Cyprus to appear in an Armed Forces Showcase for the UN troops stationed there. Gordie Tapp was the master of ceremonies, and the others included Tommy Hunter and the Rhythm Pals, dear beloved fiddler Al Cherny, Québécoise chanteuse Daniele Dorice, Peter Appleyard, the Lounsbury Sisters with their Flaming Batons, Bert Niosi's orchestra and the announcer Alan Maitland, later Fireside Al from *As It Happens.* The show was called *Hits and Mistletoe.*

We were in Cyprus to entertain the troops, but after a couple of days I realized our *real* reason for being there was to talk to the guys, to give them a bit of home. One day Gordie Tapp and I climbed a ladder to the top of a UN magazine where a young soldier was standing guard. We talked to him for a while, then I took his binoculars to view the hills beyond. As I scanned the area, I saw four guns pointed at me. I told Gordie, and we immediately ran down the ladder.

Some of the troops were stationed in outposts and couldn't attend the show since they worked twenty-four-hour shifts. We split up into three groups and went out to meet the boys. Being an army brat, I was very much aware of rank, so I donned a UN private's cap, hoping to make everyone feel equal. I sat in the front of the jeep beside the commanding officer, and we headed for Famagusta. As we approached the outpost, all the soldiers were standing at attention and singing "Farewell to Nova Scotia" for me. I stood up in the jeep, with tears streaming down my face at this moving tribute. We mingled with the guys,

I knew the words and the music, but not a sound was heard from Catherine. I didn't understand . . . I mean, this wasn't my first TV show. What went wrong? Stage fright, they told me. It only happened to me once, but what a Christmas memory.

W E MOVED TO HALIFAX, NOVA SCOTIA, WHEN I was twelve years old. I was in the choir at St. Catherine's Church and we rehearsed Christmas music for weeks. I was to sing several solos. I was having my bath on Christmas Eve at about seven o'clock and I noticed red spots all over my body. I called to my father and asked him what they could be. He said I had measles. I refused to believe it. I had had measles three times before I was three, and this was my *eighth* bout. I should have written to the *Guinness Book of World Records.* I insisted on going to mass anyway and I sang the chorus work *and* the solos, sweating all the way because I never took my coat off during the whole two-and-a-half-hour service. I don't know if anybody caught measles from me, but I was hell-bent on getting to midnight mass! I spent the rest of the holidays in bed.

By then I was taking singing lessons and was singing for anybody and everybody who wanted a singer cheap — no pay. I sang for the Rotary Club, the Lions Club, the Knights of Columbus, the Charitable Irish, the Home for Unwed Mothers, the orphans and the Home for the Mentally Disturbed. I was taken there by a wonderful man who was a Knight of Columbus, Ron Wallace, the current mayor of Halifax.

The first time I sang for the mentally ill people, someone sang who came from all parts of Canada, and we talked about home and family and loneliness during this festive season.

We went inside a tent and were treated to goodies from their Christmas packages sent from wives, mothers and lovers, while my Christmas album played "I'll Have a Blue Christmas" in the background. It's a memory I'll always cherish, their sharing and their generosity. That day I think I had a better understanding of what our boys really had to do in Cyprus and how they longed to be home with their loved ones. We, the entertainers and crew, were the lucky ones. We would be home for Christmas in a few days.

I'VE ALWAYS THOUGHT CHRISTMAS IS FOR children; after all, we are celebrating His birthday. When our daughter, Kelley, was very small, I went out and bought whimsical Christmas decorations — mice, clocks and little horses made of felt — and I made strings of popcorn and cranberries. Anything, in fact, went on the tree that wasn't made of glass, except, of course, for the rows and rows of lights. I thought that just in case the tree toppled, nobody, especially our three-year-old, would get hurt.

Donald secured the tree to the base, but he is not your average handyman (in fact he once told me that a vocational guidance test judged him to have a mechanical aptitude far below the average). The tree — lights, decorations and all — fell over three times that Christmas. I've put the tree in the stand ever since.

When Kelley was a little older, I told her the real meaning of Christmas, and I always had a crèche in the living room by the tree. Kelley would take guests by the hand, lead them into the "booful room" and re-tell the Christmas story in her own terms: "See the muvver Mary, the baby Jesus and the father Joe-fuss."

We have often celebrated Christmas in our country house a short distance north of Toronto. It's different and takes a little more organization, moving all the tree trimmings from one house to the other, but it's certainly worth it. I did make a concession and bought a blue-and-white crèche just for the country. The nicest thing about a country Christmas is going out in the back field, finding the perfect tree and chopping it down yourself. At dusk there's a stillness in the air and a deep quiet all around. The moon is bright and the sky clear, and I love the smell of the fresh-cut tree. We bring the tree inside, stand it up and let the branches spread out and fall overnight.

When we first got the country house, our next-door neighbours gave us a tiny fir tree less than half a metre high as an anniversary present. We planted it that spring, and in its early days it reminded me of the story of the scraggly Christmas tree that no one ever wanted. But as the years have gone by, it has grown into a magnificent specimen taller than our house. Last year I decided to put lights on it. I went up on the roof with forty-five metres of lights and a five-metre pole with a nail tacked on the end of it and, remembering my days with the Calgary Stampede, tried to lasso those lights onto the tree. Donald wanted to book a cherry picker instead. As he stood helplessly by at the foot of the tree, fearing for my safety, I told him necessity *is* the mother of invention, fixed the lights to the nail, whirled the long pole and went into my calf-roping act. The lights are still on the tree, awaiting our next Christmas.

In the days after Christmas we take the snowshoes out and go for a stomp through the back fields and then have a toboggan ride through the trails in the bush beside our house. One New Year's Eve we joined a party for cross-country skiing. Donald thinks of cross-country skiing as a form of penance, like crawling on your knees at Ste-Anne-de-Beaupré. My brother, René, had a camera and took a picture of Donald just to prove that he actually participated in the affair. The flash made Donald fall flat on his back, and the still night air turned blue.

One Christmas we had a sleigh ride provided by some neighbours down the road, with all their children and grandchildren along. We bundled my mother and her sister, my aunt Jeanne, up in blankets and went round the farmers' fields singing Christmas music and pushing each other off into the snow, laughing all the way. The age range went from two to well past eighty. We all had a good time except my husband, who was anxious to get home, get warm and get food. (I think he was just jealous because he can't sing!)

◄ CHRISTMAS IN THE COUNTRY IS SOMETHING EVERYONE SHOULD TRY AT LEAST ONCE, EVEN IF IT MEANS RENTING A ROOM AT AN INN. THERE IS AN OLD-FASHIONED MOOD TO IT THAT JUST CAN'T BE DUPLICATED IN THE CITY

➤ The town of St-Joseph, New Brunswick, about halfway between Moncton and Sackville, is a real-life Canadian Christmas card in the dying light of day

Everybody ended up at our house, trying to get warm in front of the log fire, sipping hot chocolate and diving into a huge vat of chili I had cooked all day. Unfortunately, I forgot to add the chili powder. Our friends were very polite and ate it anyway. I knew something was missing — it certainly didn't taste right — but it didn't hit me till the following morning. We have all laughed about it ever since.

My mother always spent Christmas with us when she moved to Toronto after my father died. Sometimes my brother and his son would come for brunch and share the day with us, open their stockings, enjoy their presents and wait for the feast later.

A dear friend I'd gone to school with, Penelope, had a children's clothing shop in the Beaches area of Toronto, and just before Christmas one year Penelope and I spent the evening cutting out large pieces of dark green, light green and red felt and making stockings for everyone in my family, including the cats. We decided to decorate them all differently to reflect their owners' individual interests and foibles. The cats got quilted satin stockings filled with catnip. Kelley was taking figure skating at the time, so hers was a large, pale green skating boot complete with white blade and bells attached where the laces would be. Gerry, Kelley's nanny, got a stocking in bright red, her favourite colour, with two orange horses with black manes, because she loves the races. My brother, René, was working for an airline at the time, so we made Snoopy out of black and white felt, complete with brown helmet, and placed him in a wooden frame to illustrate my brother's love of photography. My mother adored cats and antique dolls, so we attached an old-fashioned doll to the front of her stocking and surrounded it with cats. My brother's son, Christopher, loved soccer, so we made a soccer ball and included candy bars on it to illustrate his other great love. We made a felt dove of peace for Donald's stocking. I can't remember why we chose it. I guess it was easier than making cutouts of all the foods he loves to eat. (If that were the case, we'd still be sewing the stocking because the only food my husband can't abide is parsnips.)

My stocking had musical notes (what else!) and an angel, referring to my earlier albums, and in one corner a small piece of mincemeat pie. The previous Christmas I had used the microwave oven to warm the pie and left it in just a little too long. When the assembled guests took their first bites, they burned their tongues and nearly lost their dentures.

The stockings may stay the same, but over the years I have added to the tree decorations: wooden angels, trains, toy soldiers, colourful wooden carts filled with tiny presents. This past year, I brought from the Black Forest in Germany beautiful miniature brass hangings; walnut shells made into tiny, ornate clocks; parasols; and pearl-studded mirrors. But the special treat was finding glass clip-on birds with angel-hair tails, the kind that adorned our Christmas tree when I was a little girl, still made by the same German company.

Sometimes, because of schedules, I don't get home until Christmas Eve. Such was the case a few years ago, so I started making plans very early. I had purchased a lot of presents before I left to do the play I was in. I even bought a very sophisticated fake apricot-coloured tree (yes, I said apricot) to match the walls of our living room. It had long branches heavily laden with artificial snow, and all the decorations were in the same range of colours: all kinds of apricot and brown birds, delicate fabric roses, strands of pearls and lots of pinky-orange angels heralding the coming birth.

While I was away, the owner of the store came to our house, painstakingly inserted A into B, assembled the tree and decorated it for me. When my friend Nancy Mazeika came for a visit, she just looked at it, shook her head and said it was the absolute manifestation of my stress. Kelley rolled her eyes and announced that no matter what, from now on, we'd have a normal, real, *green* tree decorated with her beloved mice. Donald looked at this pastel synthetic vision and said he thought it was the dress Cher had worn to the previous year's Academy Awards. Well, it had looked great in the store window.

Sometimes it's hard to find the perfect present for someone. I always have a hard time finding a present for Nancy's husband, Al. I mean, how many ties can a man wear? But one day I called Nan, very excited, saying I had found *the* gift for Al . . . a brass razor. There was a long pause on the other end of the phone, followed by simultaneous shrieks of laughter from both of us. Al Mazeika has had a beard since the day I met him almost twenty years ago and wears it to this day. I gave him the razor anyway; he said he thought he could use it to scale fish.

M USIC IS SUCH AN INTEGRAL PART OF Christmas, and I've been lucky enough to work with several symphony orchestras. I have fond memories of playing the triangle in Haydn's *Toy* Symphony with the Toronto Symphony, and one year I did the big Stelco-sponsored Christmas concert with the Hamilton Philharmonic, with happy, bubbly children and an audience that sang along with me. Then there was the Edmonton Symphony, conducted by the very innovative Peter Nero, who combined classical music with break dancing! But the most memorable by far was a guest appearance with the Winnipeg Symphony, a live concert taped for television. I was singing "White Christmas" and *forgot the lyrics* halfway through! Can you imagine? It's not as if you can *fake* one of the best-loved and most easily recognized Christmas songs in the world. Luckily the audience had started to sing along with me, so it wasn't a total disaster, but it's certainly one Christmas show I'll never forget. The lyrics of Irving Berlin's song are engraved in my mind in letters of fire.

PART 21

A Voice for Christmas

By W. O. Mitchell

M A YELLED AT ME FROM THE KITCHEN, BUT I ran out the back door; I wasn't waiting to put on my scarf, or coat, or toque, not till I'd told Jake. Just the way I was I ran — snow to my knees, the whole yard staring with it, deep, the soft kind you get when she's been an open winter saving it all up for a few weeks before Christmas.

The other side of the blacksmith shop I could see our barn kind of like a real red cake with thick white icing that wasn't put on so careful. It was Christmas snow, sparkly as anything; there were a million stars caught in the roof of our hen-house alone.

She wasn't so bright in the blacksmith shop where Jake was working over the forge. He was turning the handle on the old cream separator he had made into a blower, and bending over the coals the way he was made his face sort of blush up a soft orange, like a sunset.

Looking at Jake a person wouldn't guess right off how much he's done for his country. He didn't do so bad in the Boer war; and Jake was at Vimy Ridge. He even keeps trying to get into this war. Last time was his tenth try, when he darked his hair before he went into Crocus. The fellows that take on the soldiers turned him down again. Jake says he might have known they'd smell the shoe polish some.

He looked around when I came into the blacksmith shop.

"You oughta hear, Jake!"

"Hear what?" He reached down a pair of tongs from the wall.

"About the radio. We gotta —"

"Ain't int'rested," Jake cut in on me. "You know dang fine." He stood there with the tongs hanging from the hand; he'd forgot all about the crowbar lying in the coals. "Why, if they was to take ev'ry —"

"But, Jake, we got a letter from the —"

"— squawkin' radio in this here country, and lay 'em end to end, and give me a holt of a axe —"

"But we got a letter from —"

"No wonder they ain't bin a decent crop in years — them there radio waves ripplin' and skitterin' around. The rain ain't had a chance to fall. That's —"

"But this's all about the Christmas programme where —"

"Don't tell me about no programmes. Lookit what they done to that poor fella last year — went right inta his house, broadcast what everybuddy said round the table. Couldn't let 'em eat their own Christmas dinner in peace."

"But, Jake, you don't —"

"Interference, they call it. It's interference, all right. Take this here winter — a sorta long skinny fall, that's all she is. Any snow? Not till last week. Blizzards? Nosiree bob; and there ain't gonna be none neither, not with them radios —"

"Jake, this's —"

"Why, I never fergit the winter of o' six. So cold you could see jack rabbits clear acrosst the prairie — froze. Froze in the middle of the air, height about two foot off of the ground where they leapt and got froze. One day I seen a jack kinda squatted over a rose apple bush, about three feet behind him a coyote with his feet drawed up right under him ready to spring on the jack. Come spring the jack he unfroze first; gotta head start on the coyote that way and —"

"Jake, it's about my —"

"Same winter the Fister boys caught them a young coyote; trained him to howl tenor so's he could carry the harmony while —"

"Jake, it's about my dad!"

"Huh? What about yer dad?"

"We're gonna talk with him, Christmas Day, like — remember how they went clear acrosst Canada so's kids and their folks could talk with their fathers that's overseas?"

"But you ain't —"

"I sure am, Jake. I got the letter right here saying about what we gotta do."

Jake grabbed the letter right out of my hand. He looked at her a minute. "We gotta be in that there stoodio four o'clock Christmas?"

"Yep, Jake."

"And we're gonna hear yer dad?"

"Yep!"

"Talk with him?"

I said yes with my head.

"Chrissmuss!"

Up till we got that letter I'd figured on getting tube skates and a hockey stick for Christmas. When I knew I was going to talk with my dad in England, I didn't care if I used bob skates till I was as old as Jake. And Ma — take that night when I asked for another piece of bread and butter and peanut butter; she just looked across the kitchen table at me, her dark eyes starey and wide. I figured for a minute the coal oil lamp was

doing things to her mouth — flickering like a yellow moth's wing, making her mouth like that. Then her chin went, sort of, and she out the kitchen.

Jake he looked up from where he was hunched over his saskatoon pie.

"I didn't do nothing," I said.

"Wimmen is kinda soft."

"But, why did she hafta —?"

"Wasn't nothin' you done; the peanut butter done it."

"Peanut butter?"

Kind of absent-minded Jake had his eye on the butter dish. "Hayin' time or harvest she always brung lunch out to me an' yer dad. Yer dad was always fussy about peanut butter sanwiches."

A purple saskatoon berry out of his pie was jiggling in the stubble at the corner of Jake's mouth. While he fumbled with his knife, he stared down at the oilcloth. "Always had to bring three or four extry fer yore dad." He pushed the butter dish nearer him with his knife, next his pie plate. "Wimmen always gotta blow the little things up twicet their size — ain't the stuff in wimmen they is in men. Not like — like in us, Kid." He'd finished buttering his pie; I never knew Jake to eat butter on pie before; I never knew anyone to eat butter on saskatoon pie.

NEXT DAY AFTER WE GOT THE LETTER TELLING about talking to my dad, I could hardly wait to see Violet and the other kids; Violet she's from England, and stays with Mrs. Tincher till this war is over. I was dressing fast as I could by the kitchen stove, and it cracking its knuckles to beat anything. Jake was coming in and out while he did the morning chores; Ma making pancakes. I never wanted to get to school so much in all my life. Nobody in our district was ever broadcasters before.

I was so excited I almost forgot to go out and feed Milk. Milk she's what you call a squirt cat; all the time she sits next to Jake when he's milking, and she waits for him to send her a squirt — so she's a squirt cat. She's grey, and death on gophers in summer, and was going to have some kittens. I'm fussy about Milk; my dad gave her to me just before he went to fight, and he said to take good care of her. Her going to have kittens would be just like getting a bunch of presents from my dad, and him way over in England — Christmas kittens.

After I'd fed Milk, I headed for school, Mr. Churchill Two ahead of me. It was his first snow, and he sure liked it — bouncy he went, the way Jake says he saw a jack go. I guess he figured it made him go faster. He'd stick his nose deep in the snow, and push her along, then lift his head and chew like anything, and shake his head, and come running back to me. He was fussy about the prairie in winter; anybody would be, with her all lard-white the way she was, stretching wide to where the sky started, soft grey the way it is in winter. You could hardly tell where the prairie quit; I never heard her so still

— clean, cold, still.

Coming home from school I noticed it wasn't so still; she'd turned whispery with the wind that had started her smoking — thin snow smoke breathing off the drifts here and there across the prairie. Over the horizon the sky wasn't soft grey any more. Dark.

That was when I began to get worried for fear something might turn up to keep us from talking with my dad. What if it came a bad blizzard and we couldn't get into town with the roads all snowed up?

I asked Jake about it later on, after supper. "Don't you worry about no blizzards," Jake said. "They ain't gonna be no more blizzards like we useta have. Take o' six — there was the year fer blizzards. Old Man Froomby dang near went west that year. Stormin' so bad he strung a rope from his back shed to the barn so's he wouldn't lose hisself goin' from the shack to the barn to feed the stock. He folla'd the rope all right — got hisself lost when he let go the rope and stepped inside the barn."

"How come, Jake?"

"Wasn't no barn; wind took her right offa the door and blowed her clear inta the next township. Old Man Froomby froze so bad before they found him the doc had to lop off his right leg."

"What if she blows up another like that, between now and Christmas, Jake?"

"She won't."

"But what if —?"

"Look," he said, "don't you worry none. Ye're gonna talk with yer dad if me and you and yer ma gotta pile onto Baldy's back to git into Crocus fer that there train. I tell you she'll never be like she was in o' six."

I guess she was awful in o' six.

Jake was right, in a way; we had some real fine weather. But about three days before Milk's Christmas kittens were born was when Jake started being wrong.

This time the sky along the horizon didn't clear up; the thermometer started going down, and she kept going down. The wind, first she was just long soft sound you couldn't tell exactly where from, and each day she was yelling a little longer and a little louder. Three days before Christmas she was telling everybody across the prairies they weren't going to live forever, crying like anything in the weather stripping of our storm door, licking up the snow and firing it in your face so hard you had to shut your eyes when you were facing into it. Ma wouldn't let me go to school the last day before Christmas holidays. Jake kept right on saying she'd never be like she was in o' six.

Nights I listened to the wind howling around our eaves; it didn't look to me like we were going to make her in to take that train in Crocus, even if Jake said we would — not if she got worse.

And she did; the thermometer in our back shed said fifty below just before I went to bed the night before Christmas Eve.

I lay there with my eyes right open in the dark. I couldn't sleep, thinking how we might not be able to get into town; I couldn't have slept anyway with the wind grabbing my bed and shaking it to beat anything, and the whole house creaking loud, and Jake in his room next to me. High over the blizzard I could hear Jake's snore, just the part where somebody grabs his throat, and he can't get his breath out.

It was Jake's snore started me thinking about Milk. Jake's snore always starts out sort of purry. I got to thinking about Milk and her kittens, just born. With that blizzard on, they could easy freeze to death up in our loft; it was full of cracks for the wind to get at them. My father told me to look after everything while he was away, help Jake with the stock, keep the trough full, give Jake a hand with unharnessing at night. Dad, he gave me Milk; she was stock too; she was special stock. I'd hate to have her kittens freeze while I lay in a warm bed. My dad never ever let stock shift for themselves.

I got up.

In the kitchen Mr. Churchill Two came out from behind the stove and jumped all over me while I got the coal scuttle and the lantern. He was too young for blizzards yet.

The wind slammed both me and the shed door against the back of the house. I couldn't get it shut again. The lantern flickered, nearly went out; I stuck it in the scuttle and headed for the barn.

Even with the wind at my back it was hard to get any breath; she was choking cold, kind of grabbing at the back of your throat the way an icicle sticks to a person's fingers. Between the house and the barn I only fell down once, but I got right up with snow down my neck, and up my sleeves. The lantern was still going.

I MADE HER TO THE BARN, GOT THE PEG turned in the door and opened her just enough to slip inside. I never thought I could be so fussy about a barn's inside. She was friendly warm, and sparkling something fierce with the frost growing everywhere; the walls and stalls and rafters winked and blinked and twinkled in the lantern light; some places on the roof she hung two inches thick, tufted — diamond grass. The knobs on Baldy's hames, the horsehair hanging on a nail by his stall, were crusted white with it; Eglantine and Baldy really had Christmas decorations.

Baldy didn't look round at me; Eglantine was down, she didn't pay any attention to me.

Up in the loft Milk raised her head, and stared green at me, without blinking. She didn't kick any while I put her kittens in the scuttle; they hardly moved at all. I didn't put Milk in till I got down from the loft; she'd follow me if I had her kittens.

The blizzard wind got me right by the throat, grabbed my nose, needled my eyes; going back to the house I was going to have to walk into her. It'd be real handy, I was thinking, if a person had their eyes and mouth in the back of their head. With the snow way past my knees I couldn't walk backward; all I could do was squeeze my eyes tight, put my head down, and try and get my breath with that wind doing its best to blind me and choke me.

EVERY ONCE IN A WHILE I'D STOP, TURN around, and get my eyes opened. The lantern was out. I didn't care; all it could do was show me that stingy snow, alive with the wind lifting it and driving it against me, around me, down on me.

I wasn't getting worried any, not seeing the house yet; Jake always says she seems twice as far when you can't tell how close you're getting to where you're headed for. Only thing got me bothered some was the way my legs were getting heavier all the time; a person wouldn't think taking a walk between a house and a barn in a blizzard could be such hard work.

It wasn't till the second time I stumbled, and the snow threw me, that I got het up. Pushing into the snow with my mitt, I hit something hard, and long. I took another feel at her, then felt some more in the drift around. There were all kinds of them.

I stood still, the wind pushing hard on my back with both hands. I was by our wood pile. Our wood pile's on the other side of our house to what the barn is. I was feeling sort of scairt.

I was lost.

I lit out again, and I was thinking about how Old Man Froomby lost his leg in o' six. I was thinking how a person's feet and hands get cold even when they got shoe-packs and mitts on and are mostly warm from exercise like I was.

She was taking too long to get to the house; I wasn't getting any nearer I was sure. I stopped. I took my mitt off, felt in the coal scuttle to see how Milk and her kittens were. I stuck my mitt on quick so I wouldn't lose it.

I didn't know till later why I couldn't feel Milk and her kittens.

My legs were sinking right up to my knees in snow and I headed into her again. For all I knew now I was walking right through that black stinging blizzard, out onto the bald-headed prairie where Ma and Jake would find me in the morning — maybe not till next spring when the snow melted off.

It wasn't because I was tired I sat down. The reason I sat down, I wanted to sit down, so I sat down. I thought I'd have a little rest before I took another try at her, so I sat down for a little rest. My legs were sure glad I did it, and once I was sitting, I all of a sudden wasn't so cold any more; I'd got my second warmth.

They ought to sell snow instead of those hard mattresses; they ought to rig up some way to get the wind to sing people asleep. Lying in snow is just like in bed on a Saturday morning; just like after measles when you don't have to fight the wallpaper and the door knob and the quilt any more. Blizzards in these days wasn't so cold, Jake had said, and Jake was right.

In o' six she really was cold.

After a while I was hearing Jake's voice.

"— the year of the blue snow. Some folks claim you always git a blue shadow in snow when she's got a deep enough hole in her. That wasn't why she was blue in o' six; she was blue with cold in o' six. All the jacks acrosst the —"

"Just watch he doesn't get on those feet for a couple of days." That was Doctor Fotheringham from Crocus, and what was he doing in our house? From the foot of the bed I heard a couple of mews — big ones — then a lot of little mewings. "He'll be all right. They'll all be all right."

"Ma — Jake!"

My ma was beside me, and she was kissing me. Women are kind of soft.

After Ma had gone out with Doctor Fotheringham, Jake stayed at the foot of the bed, looking down at me.

"Well, you sure done her, didn't you?"

"My feet and hands, Jake, they —"

"Hurt like blue blazes."

"Yeah. I — they — I'm gonna —"

"Oh no you ain't. They just bin froze some. How's yer face?"

"Burny — oh Jake!"

"You ain't gonna lose nothin' — not like Old Man Froomby done. Doc thought he might take a little off of yer nose. I wouldn't let him."

"Thanks — Jake."

"I told 'm he oughta take off the head — round about the neck."

A person can always tell when Jake's kidding.

"What'd you hafta do her fer anyway?"

"I went out to get Milk and her kittens."

"You went out to git Milk and her kittens, and if it hadn't bin for Mr. Churchill Two you'd be stiffer'n a froze quarter of beef."

"Mr. Churchill?"

"Heard him whimperin' and yappin', and come down. Kitchen door was blowed open, and him runnin' to it and back again. We found you and them cats — 'bout as far as I could spit from the back shed door."

"Well, anyway it's turned out all right, Jake." He didn't answer me. "What's wrong, Jake?"

"Well, you — We ain't —" Jake quit.

"Jake, what is it?"

"I never did have no use fer them dang radios —"

"Jake!"

"Doc said you had to stay off of them feet. We —"

"Jake, I'm gonna talk to my dad!"

"Ain't nothin' we kin do about her, Kid. Doc said we could carry you downstairs fer Christmas dinner tomorra. That's all."

I didn't even turn my head away. Jake could see me all he liked. He went out.

I could see right out the bedroom window Christmas morning; Jake cleaned the frost off for me to look out. I could see our whole yard drifted with snow, the buildings bare, huddling around the edge; the windmill black against the sky. I could even see the rack, bare naked after the blizzard, wheels snow to the hubs. I wished I was dead.

I could hear them downstairs, getting dinner ready. For a while there were people going in and out the front door. I could hear them talking, but I wasn't interested; I didn't care. In the log cabin quilt Ma threw over me I counted the blue strips — faded blue; my dad's old work pants.

Mr. Churchill Two came into my room, jumped up on the bed, stood on my stomach with his head on one side, looking at me. He kissed at my nose, tried to push his face between my neck and the pillow. It didn't do any good.

I wasn't going to talk to my dad over in England.

"Merry Christmas!" Jake looked like he'd et a sunset. I said Merry Christmas too; I'd already said it to him four times.

"Git yer socks on. We're goin' down."

"I don't feel so much like —"

"Oh yes you do. You wanta hear yer dad, don't you?"

"Yeah, but —"

"All right, put yer arm over my shoulder."

Jake's strong; he lifted me like I was a light oat bundle; we started down the stairs.

Just before we got in the front room Jake stopped. "Now take her easy, Kid," he said.

There was a kitchen chair by the geraniums; there was a fellow I never saw before, sitting in it. He had earphones on him; he was sitting in front of our kitchen table; he was fiddling with the front of a big black box full of dials like on a radio. He was saying:

"Three — four — hello. Hungerdunger of Hungerdunger — Hungerdunger — Hungerdunger and MacCormack. One two three four — testing. One two three four — testing."

J AKE TOLD ME AFTERWARD HOW HE'D DONE IT. He got on our phone the morning after I got lost in the blizzard; he phoned to the radio in the city, and he asked them why didn't they come to our place and broadcast like they did with that Christmas dinner programme last year. The fellow at the other end said no. Jake he argued, and the fellow said no again. That was when Central told Jake he couldn't use language like that through her switchboard.

Jake said he was sorry, and then he told the fellow how I'd gone out into the blizzard to get a cat my father gave me before he went overseas. The fellow said that was too bad, that it would make a real good story for over the air — he said something about humans — but he still didn't think they could do her.

Central told Jake to be careful again, and Jake said he would, and he asked the fellow why they couldn't send down a rig for broadcasting from our place, and the fellow said even if they wanted to they couldn't, on account of the roads being snowed up so they couldn't get through from town. Jake didn't get a chance to say anything right away with Mrs. Abercrombie

cutting in to tell the radio fellow how her son-in-law took his wife in to have a baby in Crocus, and he made it all right with a bob-sleigh and team.

Old Man Gatenby, listening in too on the party line, he said sure they could get through; he did her to bring back the Christmas tree he forgot. Mrs. Pete Springer said Pete could easy meet the train and help them get their stuff out to our place. Jake said you could hardly think for all those people on our party line, making suggestions.

When he could get a word in edgewise, Jake said what if I mightn't pull through unless I heard my father's voice, and talked with him? And if they didn't send down the broadcasting rig my death would be on their head.

That was when Central chimed in and said they ought to be ashamed of themselves around that radio station if they didn't do something to save my life. The fellow said all right, you win — all of you.

There isn't anybody anywhere else in the world like Jake, or my dad, or my ma — or the folks on our party line.

We came right after the ones from Regina, and the announcer said all about me going out in the blizzard to get Milk and her kittens, and he said about Mr. Churchill Two, and I sat there with my stomach the size of my fist, only tighter, and my throat getting wobblier and wobblier, waiting to hear my father. Jake he was on the edge of his chair, leaning forward; he had a hold of the chair hard; I could see the veins standing out — blue earthworms crawling over the backs of his hands. I never saw Ma's eyes look the way they were looking then.

The announcer quit. For a minute all you could hear was a sort of beating, wavy sound out of the radio.

"Hello — hello."

"Dad!"

"You all right, son?"

"I — I'm fine. You — hello Dad! It — Milk's fine too.

"Jake he — oh Dad!"

"You looking after your mother?"

I couldn't say anything; all I could do was listen while my ma talked to him, and he told her he'd got his parcels. And then he said:

"Jake there?"

Jake's mouth was part open; his eyes looked real tired — old tired — like they'd been looking against prairie sun too long.

"Jake."

Jake's mouth came shut. "Me? Why, shore, I —"

"You looking after those folks of mine?"

"Yore damn pertootin' I am!" The fellow with the earphones dug Jake in the side. "Huh? Oh — guess a fella ain't sposed to say, 'yer damn per —' All right — all right."

"Understand you've had a rough winter."

"Hell no," Jake bust out without paying any attention to the radio fellow. "Little touch of wind odd times — some snow. Nothin' atall. She ain't bin a patch on o' six. She'll never be like she was in o' six agin."

PART 22

A Few Friends Drop In

CHRISTOPHER PLUMMER'S CHRISTMAS

CHRISTMAS IS ALWAYS THERE SOMEWHERE DEEP INSIDE me, and all through the long year I wait impatiently for it to surface. As it approaches, memories and fond feelings tug gently at my sleeve and they take me with them, back to when I was a boy . . . and I find myself staring, quite unashamedly, into the very core of all my Christmases.

The best were in Montreal, where I grew up, engulfed in snowdrifts as high as the ocean waves. Little blue lights on all the trees shone at night up the steep streets on the sides of the "mountain," reflecting the white cliffs crowned by the lighted giant cross . . . the sentinel at the top. The deep snow had silenced the city and there was a holy peace about those dark blue nights I shall never forget. Then, on Sherbrooke Street, I would stand for hours staring at the rooftops of the Château Apartments and its ominous neighbouring church and watch the gargoyles brooding over their turrets — at this time of year no longer menacing but looking somewhat surprised, slightly silly and rather dear, with long icicles hanging from their snarling jaws like spiky beards or thin, clear mint sticks.

I remember skating home on Christmas Eve to my

⋀ *OLD QUEBEC CITY, WHICH BECAME A UNITED NATIONS WORLD HERITAGE SITE IN 1985, IS ESPECIALLY PICTURESQUE AT CHRISTMASTIME. LEFT, ST. JOHN'S, NEWFOUNDLAND*

grandmother's country house on the frozen "Lake of Two Mountains," the hills of Oka behind us (outlined in the clear dark ice under our blades), goading us on as we raced home hungry as wolves, then the roaring fires and smiling dogs with brilliantly coloured ribbons round their necks drooling expectantly for some rare festive treats. We'd have a very grown-up dinner with all the trimmings . . . my first black-tie (compulsory) and my grandmother's faithful, aged gardener (dear old Louis Brunet, my bestest friend, who as a child had been in service to my great-grandfather) now dressed in his best "bib and tucker" gracefully pouring the cider and wines. I remember Christmases up north at St-Sauveur and Ste-Marguerite: the smell of freshly baked *galette au beurre* and *pain chinoix* wafting up the slopes toward us, luring us home. High on the hills we rested on our poles and listened to the church bells below us, and we could just make out little dots of people (habitants) returning home to early dinners: old men in gaily painted sleighs drawn by horses . . . the same old men, the same colourful sleighs, the same horses with which the famous Seven had insisted on complementing their landscapes. I remember one ribald Christmas years later, when, soused to the

▼ Catherine and actor Gordon Pinsent, a family friend for many years, make merry at a Christmas gathering at our Toronto home, below left. With thoughts of Gretzky and Lemieux in mind, the young lad, below, is ready for a little game of pre-Christmas pickup hockey

gills, we bashed down those very slopes on our skis at hair-raising speed, immaculately attired in full evening dress! (I've never seen *that* on film.) And there were those very treasured times I had as a boy, reading aloud to my grandfather from Stephen Leacock's "Hoodoo McFiggin's Christmas" and others

of that ilk . . . and both of us laughing so hard I couldn't go on.

Most Yuletides of mine were wrapped in music. There was music everywhere — French carols old as the hills, glorious concerts in Notre-Dame Cathedral with the full orchestra, organ and boys' choirs, all the way up through the Pavarotti years, the Russian chorales, Elizabeth Schwarzkopf (surely Stormin' Norman's cousin) delighting with her German hymns. Not just Christmas music but most music fitted the occasion. Put on the third movement of Saint-Saën's Fourth Piano Concerto, for instance, and by God if it isn't "While Shepherds Watched Their Flocks by Night" played backward!

And you must remember, Don, Andrew Allan's quite marvellous radio production of *Christmas at Dingley Dell* (I'm certain we were both in it) and the bubbly, witty, lush, twinkling score Lucio Agostini composed for it, which has come as close to the spirit of Charles Dickens as anything musically I've ever heard.

No matter how far my gypsy wanderings have taken me, all my Christmases seem to work like a dream. They work a treat in Gloucestershire (open fires on Cotswold stone . . . cider with Rosie, anyone?). They work in Madrid, London, Vienna . . . even in Rome. And now, at home in Connecticut, boy, do they work! My dear, long-suffering wife, "Fuffie," has, God bless her, brilliantly carried on the tradition with fun, style, imagination . . . all accomplished with maddening but breathtaking ease. But in Florida? Or California? Not quite! Pretty unnatural and hysterically funny Christmases have been spent in both spots, trying mightily to make it seem as if we were somewhere else. Much too much glitter, as if the blinding sun was not enough. Far too many decorations — far too much excess — rampant kitsch! It is not easy to conjure up one's usual cozy Christmas as one stands gazing at the Pacific, "silent, upon a peak in Darien." Basil and Ouida Rathbone, grand party throwers at holiday time in the 1930s and 1940s (the British Gerald Murphys of Hollywood), insisted on hiring machines to cover their house and entire compound in artificial snow to remind them of homier times. Well, I don't blame 'em a bit. And yet, when you come to think of it, the hometown of our First Born was a tad tropical (wasn't it?) to say the least.

The one thing I cannot understand or sympathize with are the people who actually run from Christmas like lemmings to some silly hotel somewhere with lousy room service to get away, as they keep shouting, from its growing commercialism. So what? Let it be commercial, if it must. I care not a fig just so long as it doesn't go away. Let the presents be bigger and better . . . louder and funnier . . . why not? Let's stay where the action is, right in the midst of it. Let's not be ashamed of being old-fashioned about it; let's not be embarrassed by its romance. Let its spirit ride free, for let me tell you, when it's over and the embers die down, the world has lost a friend, and in the days that follow, the blood is drained from it . . . its face becomes a mask of bleakness that languishes and lingers till the first crocus comes, the last leaf falls and then the heart begins to race. That old longing returns . . . the candles are lit . . . we take up our vigil . . . and suddenly that miraculous, joyous day is once more upon us, and I whisper my secret to the star that warmed some ancient, distant desert . . . that no matter how old I become, I will *never, never* grow out of it.

Norman Jewison's
Christmas in Wales

Dixie shouted over the loudspeaker she installed at our farm: "It's Charlie Farquharson on the phone again!" "Jesus, Dixie! Tell him I'm out of the country. Tell him I'm dying of pneumonia. Tell him I'm dead." Dixie, who never lies on the telephone, replied, "Hold on, Don, he's coming." I staggered up the hill, climbed the fence and almost beat the dog to the kitchen door. Dixie handed me the phone. "Yeah, Don, how ya doin'?" Don Harron always talks in a quiet low whisper when he's playing Don Harron: "Did I get you at a bad time?" he asked softly. "No, it's okay." I coughed. "I was outside in the field across from the kitchen trying to — no, it's okay." I was really coughing now. "I've got this terrible cold, and I'm in the middle of editing my new movie in Toronto . . ." "I know how busy you always are," he purred. "Catherine performed three shows this week with walking pneumonia . . . a lot of it going around." "Yes, there is." I snuffled and blew my nose hard.

I knew he wasn't going to give me any sympathy and understanding. "I'm putting together another book," he continued. "It includes various Canadians reminiscing about memorable Christmases they've experienced. I'd like you to be a part of it; I know how busy you must be with your film and everything, but maybe if I gave you my fax number . . ."

When someone gives you a fax number, it's all over. You're finished. The fax machine is waiting in his or her house, waiting for you to send it something. Waiting. Waiting. Like a mother-in-law, tapping her foot. I coughed and hacked my way through two more days in the editing room, always thinking about that fax machine . . . humming quietly . . . waiting. Don left another message at the office after three days.

So, here I am. It's 2:30 a.m. Coughing and shaking with fatigue, I will try to recall the events surrounding the Jewison family's most memorable Christmas.

It was London, 1972. A rather eccentric American screenwriter, Bob Carrington, called us up and invited Dixie, myself and our three kids, Kevin, Michael and Jenny, to spend Christmas in Wales with him and some friends. They had rented

a castle for the Christmas season. "A real castle?" I asked. "Yeah, with a moat, dungeons, tower and everything," he said. "Don't worry, there's lots of room and a section has been modernized. Boaty Boatwright's coming with her kids; it'll be a blast."

Dixie felt the children would enjoy a truly English Christmas in Wales, so we packed up — presents, gifts, hampers — and piled onto the train for Swansea. In one small wicker basket we smuggled a six-week-old Yorkshire terrier pup. He was so quiet, I thought he had smothered. But Jenny never knew he was with us. It was an overnight train ride to Swansea, then on to Manorbier Castle by car. There it stood, shrouded in mist, a storybook castle rising out of the Welsh moors. The castle was owned by Lord and Lady Dunsany, who lived in Ireland. Manorbier Castle was Norman, dating back to the eleventh century. Bob Carrington had rented it for the winter season for five pounds a month. I guess nobody else wanted it. In the summer it was open for tourists, and wax effigies were dressed and put on display.

When we arrived, the pup was immediately hidden in one of the bathrooms, far away from Jenny. Christmas Eve, we all bundled up and headed for the local pub in the village. Crowded, smoke-filled, fireplace roaring, it was a scene out of a Dickens novel. Red, round faces, shaggy dogs, everyone staring at the crazy American and Canadian group who had rented the castle.

As closing time approached, someone started to sing a Christmas carol. The voices rose in unison. My God it's true, the Welsh can really sing. At one point, they looked over at our table and someone shouted, "A carol from the visitors!" I turned to Michael, our ten-year-old: "Go ahead, Mike, give 'em 'Silent Night.'" Michael was lifted up and put in the centre of the table. To our surprise, he faced the crowd and began to sing without any hesitation. It was a great moment; the noisy room gradually grew silent as the sweet, young voice of a boy soprano singing

Silent night, holy night,
All is calm, all is bright

filled the room. He looked like Oliver Twist up there. Eyes filled with tears at the innocence and hope. Everyone joined in on the second chorus and we were a hit with the crowd. Arriving back at the castle much later, the children were put to bed and Bob Carrington told them not to be frightened if they heard horses' hooves on the cobblestone courtyard during the night. It was just the ghost of the young prince returning to find his princess who had thrown herself from the tower some four hundred years ago when she heard he was killed in battle. "You mean this place is haunted?" "Of course," Bob replied. "All these old castles have ghosts." The kids were impressed but not convinced.

Christmas morning was spent around the tree, giving and receiving gifts. A note on the tree was for Jenny. It instructed her to count to ten, turn around three times, then go out the main door of the castle and look by the well in the centre of the courtyard. Everyone fell silent as she began to comply with the mysterious instructions. We followed this tiny eight-year-old as she struggled to open the huge castle door and go out into the empty, misty courtyard. In her nightie and slippers, she ran across to the well and there, on the cobblestones, hidden behind the well, was sitting this tiny, shivering Yorkshire terrier puppy. The joy, the tears, the ecstasy that poured out of Jenny as she swept the pup up into her arms were immense. It affected all of us. Naturally, she called the pup Wales. He lived with her and the family for the next fourteen years.

It was, without a doubt, our favourite Christmas. We feasted on roast goose and red cabbage in the Great Hall. Later on Christmas Day, a breeches buoy was rigged from the top turret on the drawbridge to a tree some three hundred metres away. The boys and men took turns roaring through the air in the canvas bucket high above the moat and raging seas. Searches for ghosts in the dungeons, tramping across the misty moors, mediaeval banners hanging in the main dining hall, it was just one of those Christmases that should have been filmed. But then, we all have our memories and maybe they play better in our mind's eye.

BARBARA HAMILTON'S ORPHAN'S CHRISTMAS

CANADA KNOWS THIS WONDERFUL WOMAN FOR HER many cross-country tours as the star of *Spring Thaw* and her unforgettable portrayal of Marilla Cuthbert in the musical *Anne of Green Gables*. But back in 1951 Barbara was trying out her luck in New York and working in the luggage department of Bloomingdale's while waiting for that big Broadway break. Her father sent her a cheque for Christmas; it offered her the option of coming home for the holiday or staying in New York for a couple of months on the proceeds of the cheque. Barbara decided to stay in New York, an orphan for Christmas.

A *Spring Thaw* alumnus, Alfie Scopp, told her to call up Leslie Neilson (Yukon Erik's little brother), who was giving a Christmas tree decorating party for theatrical types at loose ends on Christmas Eve. Barbara was too shy to make the call, so Alfie phoned for her, and the next thing Barbara knew after a tough day in Bloomingdale's was Leslie Neilson urging — nay, ordering — her to stop being a Canadian orphan in the big city, get over to his apartment and join her fellow thespians in throwing decorations at his tree.

When she got there, she saw a bare tree, slightly lopsided, and beside it several boxes of Christmas ornaments with names assigned to various show-biz types, the likes of Wally Cox and

Montgomery Clift. The Christmas Eve festive atmosphere dispelled her feeling of loneliness in a strange town. It was something she never forgot.

Back in Toronto, with a house of her own, Barbara organized an orphans' dinner for travelling show folk. Her annual party was for anybody from out of town visiting Toronto during Christmas, and it was a runaway success, with anywhere from sixty to one hundred grateful guests showing up. No wonder Barbara is so magnificent as Marilla, looking after that little orphan, Anne of Green Gables.

GORDON PINSENT'S JANNY-ERS

GORDON PINSENT IS THE MOST VERSATILE PERFORMER I know. He can and has done everything there is to do in our business. A lot of this versatility comes from the need to make a living in this country. That's why Canadians are so often successful in the United States and why many of them end up as executive producers: they've been involved in every aspect of a production.

Gordon *(Quentin Durgens, M.P.; The Rowdyman; A Gift to Last)* was born and grew up in Grand Falls, Newfoundland. He left there as a teenager to make his way in theatre and television, but he still has total recall of his childhood. Among other things, he remembers cowering behind the wood stove when the mummers came to his door at Christmas. Gordon calls them Janny-ers, rather than mummers, named for the two-faced Roman god Janus, who looked back into the old year and forward into the new. For that reason, Janny-ers spoke a lot of words backward. They would come to your door wearing a sheet over an old hat and ask, "Any Janny-ers in tonight?" Rich people would wear a mask with goat tails, but Gordon says nobody in Grand Falls was that rich.

Jannying has only recently come back into favour in Newfoundland. It was taboo for a while because it led to fights between Protestants and Catholics. You never knew who — a friend, a relative or a total stranger — was under those sheets. Gordon remembers his sister Hazel sitting on the knee of someone she thought was her uncle and getting a rude pinch from a complete stranger. You were expected to guess the identity of the Janny-ers; if you did, they would throw the sheet back and have a glass of rum and a piece of Christmas cake.

As a teenager, Gordon always carried his Echo harmonica with him and played it through the sheet when he went on his Jannying rounds. He would head first for the house of a girl he happened to be sweet on at the time. He was able to say saucy things to her parents because he was very good at disguising himself, and it gave him a particular thrill, in a symbolic way, to see the girl of his dreams under his sheet.

PART 23

MUSIC MAKING

➤ *THE FIRST CANADIAN CAROL WAS WRITTEN IN THE SEVENTEENTH CENTURY BY A JESUIT PRIEST, JEAN DE BRÉBEUF*

C AROLS WERE THE POP MUSIC OF THE MIDDLE Ages, but very few of them had anything to do with Christmas. They were popular because the lyrics were in the language of the people instead of church Latin. The word itself implies a folk dance in the shape of a ring. Carols have a pagan origin that involved a lot of clapping and singing and moving in circles and in grand chains like a rustic square dance. The songs celebrated any joyous event or holiday. The less raucous of them were about Christmas.

The established church felt about carols the way some contemporary authorities of the 1950s and 1960s felt about rock and roll. For seven hundred years, the church denounced carols as the work of the devil and urged its members to flee such wicked and lecherous songs, which encouraged orgiastic leaping. Such heathen dancing was considered closely allied

with witchcraft. A legend that tells of the suppression of carols is enough to curl one's hair. Twelve people gather in a churchyard on Christmas Eve and join hands as they dance and sing. The priest comes out of the church and tells them to stop. They give him a flippant reply, so the spurned priest calls down the wrath of God upon them. It registers immediately, and like the ballet dancer in the film *The Red Shoes*, the carollers find that they can't stop singing or dancing. When the priest tries to drag a young woman from the whirling group, her arm is ripped loose but the stump doesn't bleed. According to the legend, the singing and dancing went on without interruption for a whole year. (How can the circle be unbroken when an arm of one of the dancers has been stumped?) Mediaeval tourists came from all over to see the phenomenon, and the curse was not lifted until the following Christmas Eve, when the carollers went inside the church to repent, then fell down and slept for seventy-two hours.

St. Francis of Assisi gets the credit for stopping all this

The largest outdoor Christmas lights supplier in Canada is Noma Inc. The company reports more and more Canadians are switching to lower-wattage bulbs, which consume about 30 per cent less energy

nonsense and accepting carols as legitimate sacred songs. St. Francis got the Tin Pan Alleyists of his day to apply pious lyrics to the tunes of the devil in much the same way as the Salvation Army has done. Suddenly carols about God and Jesus became the hit parade of the thirteenth century. Much of this re-orienting of lyrics was applied to the Christmas story, partly because St. Francis had a particular interest in the Nativity. The crèche, as I mentioned before, was all his idea, and so was the novel idea of being kind to animals.

By the beginning of the sixteenth century, carols began losing their appeal as songs for any and all seasons and became more rigidly associated with Christmas. Along came the Puritans one hundred and fifty years later to put on the brakes, so carols went underground. Carol singing in public almost disappeared in England for two hundred years. But you can't stamp a good tune from the memories of those who love to hum them, and carols were preserved as contraband golden oldies. And among the Celts, the Welsh and Irish continued to bellow out the old tunes. However, many of the carols sung four hundred years ago have been lost, and most of what we hear today has been composed in the past one hundred and fifty years.

It's interesting to trace the origin of some better-known

carols. Good King Wenceslas was not really a king but a duke in Bohemia in the tenth century. Bohemia is part of Czechoslovakia, not Greenwich Village. Wenceslas is one of those brave souls who spread Christianity among the heathen, got martyred for his trouble and became a saint. He was murdered by his younger brother, Boleslav, as he entered a church. It seems Boleslav was upset because his brother had recently added an heir to the ducal throne. The melody of the famous carol is sixteenth century, and it feels like a jaunty military march, but the poem that describes the miracle of Wenceslas's warming footsteps is strictly nineteenth century.

The first Canadian carol, "Jesous Ahatonhia" ("Jesus Is Born"), was written in the seventeenth century by a Jesuit priest, Jean de Brébeuf, in the language of the Huron Indians. Brébeuf worked among the Hurons for fourteen years, until he was tortured to death by the Iroquois. He used a French folk song as the melody, but the words reveal his deep understanding of aboriginal culture. The three wise men became three Indian chiefs bringing the baby gifts of beaver and fox furs.

Nahum Tate wrote "While Shepherds Watched Their Flocks by Night"; the melody is borrowed from an opera by George Frideric Handel. Tate is best known for his bowdlerized re-writing of Shakespeare, giving his greatest tragedy, *King Lear*, a sappy, happy ending.

"The First Noël" and "The First Nowell" are carols that originated in sixteenth-century Cornwall with similar lyrics, but they have different tunes.

Charles Wesley wasn't too busy preaching to write "Hark! the Herald Angels Sing." Originally it had a more secular title, "Hark, How All the Welkin Rings."

"Joy to the World" was written by that great creator of hymns, Isaac Watts. The present tune was developed one hundred and twenty-five years later from Handel's *Messiah*.

Martin Luther is credited with writing the favourite carol of little folk, "Away in a Manger." The tune may be his, but the words came along much later, in 1885. Nobody is sure about the beginnings of "O Come, All Ye Faithful." One theory has it written as a Latin carol, "Adeste Fideles," in the eighteenth century; the English version seems to be nineteenth century.

The most famous carol of all, "Silent Night," has an origin that is a Hollywood scriptwriter's dream. It was written in a hurry by a parish priest of a small Austrian village when the music of the high mass couldn't be performed because the church organ had broken down on Christmas Eve. The world première of this carol, in 1818, was performed on a guitar. Maybe Hollywood hasn't bothered with this story because the carol was an immediate flop and lay forgotten for years and years. A pre-Trapp family of Austrian singers who toured Europe and the United States revived it in 1839 and made it the best-loved carol of all.

A similar fate befell "O Little Town of Bethlehem," which has almost the same origins. The minister of Holy Trinity Church in Philadelphia in 1868, Phillips Brooks, wanted to have a new carol for his congregation that year, so he brought out a poem he had written in Bethlehem three years earlier when he had visited the Holy Land. He gave the poem to his organist, and despite the pressure of time, the church musician came up with a classic. However, it, too, was a classic that was buried by neglect for the next twenty years. It was resurrected for a Christmas item in a local paper and went on to claim its rightful status as a well-loved treasure.

My particular favourite is "The Cherry Tree Carol," especially when Catherine sings it. The incident is supposed to have taken place on the flight into Egypt when the holy family was fleeing the infanticide orders of King Herod. Mary, travel-worn and desperately thirsty, has to rest under a tree to escape the heat. She sees the fruit high up in the tree and wants some. Joseph says they are out of reach, and that he will try to find water. He tells Mary rather truculently to get the one who got her with child to do the cherry picking. (Obviously the tree is a coconut palm, so what's all this about cherries? As the legend travelled north, the out-of-the-way fruit became figs, later an apple and, finally, in Britain, a cherry.) Mary asks the tree to bend its branches and it does so. In some versions the incident happens on the journey to Bethlehem and it is the voice of the pre-natal Jesus in the womb who orders the tree to bow down and offer its fruit. In another variation on this theme the miracle baby appears suddenly in Mary's lap to give the order.

W HEN WE STARTED THIS BOOK, OUR IDEA WAS simply to retain something we considered worth keeping. I don't think we realized how much of an endangered species the Canadian Christmas really is. You are probably wondering what the difference is with, say, an American Christmas. The difference arises from a decision made by a Canadian government to encourage multiculturalism among our ethnic minorities instead of edging them toward the homogeneity of a melting pot, giving up their customs from the old land and blending in with the resident majority.

As a practising comedian, I happen to be a student of dialects and an observer of the idiosyncrasies of different groups of people. I'm in favour of multiculturalism. One of the most satisfying events in the calendar year happens every June, when a phenomenon called Caravan visits Toronto, and the city is dotted with impromptu, makeshift restaurants dispensing ethnic foods of a startling diversity, along with songs and dances from the same region.

To me, this is what Canada is all about, and in these difficult years of political wrangling and division, I have found that it is the hope and expectation in the eyes of our newcomers that is one of the strongest forces for keeping this country going. However, there is a negative side to all this. The municipal vote getters and civic worriers are starting to legislate in the name of multicultural harmony. Christmas is in danger of being homogenized into a kind of generic Winterfest.

I T'S HAPPENING MOSTLY IN THE SCHOOLS. I can understand the objections to the Lord's Prayer as a piece of indoctrination. Mind you, as long as there are final exams, you cannot stop fervent prayer from passing the lips of some students. But Christmas music is in danger of being limited to "Frosty the Snowman," "Rudolph the Red-Nosed Reindeer" and "Jingle Bell Rock." Some staff members think that non-Christian children would be upset by the words of the carols.

Why not include the "Song of the Dredel" from the festival of Hanukkah and the joyous rhythms of Israeli dances like the foot-stomping hora? Why not share the joys at this time of year with other ethnic groups? The Hindus have Diwali, their own Festival of Lights, and the Sikhs celebrate Baisakhi. Instead of banning "Silent Night" and "Adeste Fideles" in our schools and cancelling the Christmas concert, why not extend the range of Yuletide music instead of reverting to censorship. Are Bach and Handel next to get the chop? And what about most of the pre-Renaissance paintings?

Oddly enough, Handel had no designs on the Christmas market on April 12, 1742, when his oratorio the *Messiah* was first played as a benefit for two Dublin hospitals. Handel chose a religious theme because his other, secular operas were banned during Lent. In 1957 Elvis Presley was banned by a lot of radio stations in the United States, not for gyrating his pelvis, not for "Blooooooooo Chrismuss without you," but for daring to include on his Christmas album some sacred songs.

Catherine and I love to wish each other *kung hei fat choy* at the Chinese New Year. Someday I hope to memorize the Chinese Christmas greeting, *kung hsi hsin nien bing chu shen tan*. Now there's a real minority, Chinese Christians! Yet they can holler "God Rest You Merry, Gentlemen" in present-day China without any guilt complex.

All colours and cultures, I believe, can enjoy the tunes we call Christmas carols without feeling proselytized. When we ask friends to celebrate with us, we don't ask for belief. As one of the parents said about the censoring of Christmas at her child's school: "Songs of love and peace about a child of love and peace can only foster love and peace." Let's have a cross-cultural musical Caravan in our schools.

Christmas, like the Roman Saturnalia, deals with the rebirth of life in the dead of winter. We never talk about the "dead" of any other season, and it is a love of life that beautiful music stirs in us. It revives us at that time of year when we need hope most of all.

"*At Christmas play and make good cheer,*
For Christmas comes but once a year"
— *Thomas Tusser,* The Farmer's Daily Diet

WHEN I THINK OF CHRISTMAS MUSIC, THE carols I recall most vividly are "Adeste Fideles" and "Il est né, le Divin Enfant" because they were the first hymns I sang. I thought they were very special because they were not sung in English. I had no idea what the words meant, but I loved singing them anyway. "Il est né" originally came from France and "Adeste Fideles" was first heard in the eighteenth century. As with any music that lasts, the strength of these carols lies in a strong melody line and good lyrics. Although the hymn "D'où viens-tu, bergère?" comes from France, I think of it as French-Canadian. Québécois in rural communities have been singing it since the seventeenth century.

CATHERINE'S CAROLS

D'OÙ VIENS-TU, BERGÈRE?

D'où viens-tu, bergère,
D'où viens-tu? (repeat first two lines)
Je viens de l'étable
De m'y promener.
J'ai vu un miracle
Ce soir arrivé.

Qu'as-tu vu, bergère,
Qu'as-tu vu? (repeat first two lines)
J'ai vu dans la crèche
Un petit enfant
Sur la paille fraîche
Mis bien tendrement.

Est-il beau, bergère,
Est-il beau? (repeat first two lines)
Plus beau que la lune,
Aussi le soleil;
Jamais dans le monde
On vit son pareil.

Rien de plus, bergère,
Rien de plus? (repeat first two lines)
Sainte Marie, sa mère,
Qui lui fait b'voir du lait
Saint Joseph, son père,
Qui tremble de froid.

➢ *CHRISTMAS MORNING*

SUNRISE GILDS A FROST-CRUSTED

WINDOW IN NOVA SCOTIA

WHEN WE DID *SINGALONG JUBILEE* IN THE 1960S, we always taped a show to be aired on Christmas Day. One year, our resident baritone and wonderful writer, Jim Bennet, penned a moving little piece called the "South Shore Carol." It's about the oxen, who often symbolize humility, caring for the Christ child in the stable.

SOUTH SHORE CAROL

CHORUS
Ox bells ring ting-a-ling-ling
Greet the morn
Jesus is born

Who hears the ox this sacred night
speak within his stall:
Hail unto the humble Child
Born the King of all (repeat)

CHORUS

Nor has any choir on earth
More holy anthem sung
Than words of praise that lowly fall
When patient beasts give tongue. (repeat)

CHORUS

For all that man his wealth employs
To greet God's earthly son
A barn resounds the greatest hymn
Unheard except by one (repeat)

Music and lyrics by Jim Bennet © Black Rum Publishing

THIS IS ONE OF MY FAVOURITE VERSIONS OF "The Cherry Tree Carol."

THE CHERRY TREE CAROL

Oh Joseph took Mary upon his right knee
Saying Mary won't you tell me when the birthday shall be.
Saying Mary won't you tell me when the birthday shall be.

The birthday shall be on that old Christmas night
When the angels in the glory rejoice at the sight.
When the angels in the glory rejoice at the sight.

Mary walked in the garden just like a little child
Saying give me some cherries for I am beguiled.
Saying give me some cherries for I am beguiled.

Then Joseph said to Mary, I'll give thee no cherries
Let the man give you cherries who did you beguile.
Let the man give you cherries who did you beguile.

Then the tree spoke
unto her and it
began to bow
Saying Mary gather
cherries from the
utter most bow.
Saying Mary gather
cherries from the
utter most bow.

I GUESS IF I HAD TO choose a personal, all-time favourite, it would be "The Holly Berry Carol." The holly berry is a symbol of Christ's blood flowing from the crown of thorns.

THE HOLLY BERRY CAROL

Oh the holly has a berry; as white as the milk.
Mary bore Jesus all wrapped up in silk.
Mary bore Jesus our Saviour to be
And the first tree in the greenwood, it was the holly.
Holly, holly
And the first tree in the greenwood, it was the holly.

Oh the holly bears a berry as black as the coal
Mary bore Jesus who died for us all
Mary bore Jesus, our Saviour to be
And the first tree in the greenwood, it was the holly.
Holly, holly
And the first tree in the greenwood, it was the holly.

Oh the holly bears a berry; as blood it is red.
Mary bore Jesus who died in our stead.
Mary bore Jesus our Saviour to be
And the first tree in the greenwood, it was the holly.
Holly, holly
And the first tree in the greenwood, it was the holly.

I KNOW "DOESN'T ANYBODY HERE KNOW IT'S
Christmas" is not a carol, but I wanted to include it. It was written by my niece when she was nine years old.

DOESN'T ANYBODY HERE KNOW IT'S CHRISTMAS

Doesn't anybody here know it's Christmas?
It's Christmas today —
Hasn't anybody here got some love to give away?
It's not tinsel or a present that I'm after or laughter today.
Just a little love will do if perhaps you need some too.
I can hear sleigh bells ringing
Children singing everywhere
But it's not for me
Don't you see I've got nobody to care
Doesn't anybody here know it's Christmas today?
Doesn't anybody here understand a word I say?
Doesn't anybody here know it's Christmas today?

Music and lyrics by Jackie Rae and
Shannon Ahearn © Jar Music Ltd.

AND HERE ARE SOME OF MY FAVOURITES
among the more popular Christmas carols.
I've sung them all many times over the years,
but I never grow tired of any one of them.

AWAY IN A MANGER

Away in a manger,
No crib for a bed,
The little Lord Jesus
Laid down his sweet head.
The stars in the bright sky
Looked down where He lay
The little Lord Jesus
Asleep on the hay.

The cattle are lowing,
The Baby awakes,
But little Lord Jesus
No crying He makes.
I love Thee, Lord Jesus;
Look down from the sky,
And stay by my side
Until morning is nigh.

Be near me, Lord Jesus,
I ask Thee to stay
Close by me for ever
And love me, I pray.
Bless all the dear children
In Thy tender care,
And fit us for heaven
To live with Thee there.

O LITTLE TOWN OF BETHLEHEM

O little town of Bethlehem,
How still we see thee lie!
Above thy deep and dreamless sleep
The silent stars go by:
Yet in thy dark streets shineth
The everlasting light;
The hopes and fears of all the years
Are met in thee tonight.

For Christ is born of Mary;
And, gathered all above,
While mortals sleep, the angels keep
Their watch of wondering love.
O morning stars, together
Proclaim the holy birth,
and praises sing to God the King,
And peace to men on earth.

O Holy Child of Bethlehem,
Descend to us, we pray;
Cast out our sin, and enter in;
Be born in us today.
We hear the Christmas angels
The great glad tidings tell,
O come to us, abide with us,
Our Lord Emmanuel.

SILENT NIGHT

Silent night! holy night!
All is calm, all is bright
Round yon Virgin Mother and Child,
Holy Infant so tender and mild,
Sleep in heavenly peace,
Sleep in heavenly peace.

Silent night! holy night!
Shepherds quake at the sight;
Glories stream from heaven afar,
Heavenly hosts sing Hallelujah,
Christ, the Saviour, is born!
Christ, the Saviour, is born!

Silent night! holy night!
Son of God love's pure light;
Radiant beams from Thy holy face,
With the dawn of redeeming grace,
Jesus, Lord, at Thy birth,
Jesus, Lord, at Thy birth.

JOY TO THE WORLD

Joy to the world! the Lord is come,
Let earth receive her king;
Let every heart prepare Him room,
And heaven and nature sing. (repeat three times)

Joy to the earth! The Saviour reigns;
Let men their songs employ;
While fields and floods, rocks, hills and plains,
Repeat the sounding joy. (repeat three times)

No more let sins and sorrows grow,
Nor thorns infest the ground,
He comes to make His blessings flow,
Far as the curse is found. (repeat three times)

He rules the earth with truth and grace,
And makes the nations prove
The glories of His righteousness,
And wonders of His love. (repeat three times)

IT CAME UPON THE MIDNIGHT CLEAR

It came upon the midnight clear.
That glorious song of old,
From angels bending near the earth
To touch their harps of gold:
"Peace on the earth, good-will to men
From heaven's all-gracious King!"
The world in solemn stillness lay
To hear the angels sing.

But with the woes of sin and strife
The world has suffered long;
Beneath the angel strain have rolled
Two thousand years of wrong;
And man, at war with man, hears not
The love song which they bring;
O hush the noise, ye men of strife,
And hear the angels sing.

And ye, beneath life's crushing load
Whose forms are bending low,
Who toil along the climbing way,
With painful steps and slow,
Look now! for glad and golden hours
Come swiftly on the wing;
O rest beside the weary road,
And hear the angels sing.

HARK! THE HERALD ANGELS SING

Hark! the herald angels sing.
"Glory to the new-born King,
Peace on earth and mercy mild,
God and sinners reconciled!"
Joyful, all ye nations, rise.
Join the triumph of the skies,
With the angelic host proclaim,
"Christ is born in Bethlehem."

REFRAIN
Hark! the herald angels sing,
"Glory to the new-born King."

Christ, by highest heaven adored,
Christ, the everlasting Lord,
Late in time behold Him come,
Offspring of a virgin's womb.
Veiled in flesh the Godhead see;
Hail, the Incarnate Deity;
Pleased as Man with man to dwell,
Jesus, our Emmanuel!

Hail, the heaven-born Prince of Peace.
Hail, the son of Righteousness!
Light and life to all He brings,
Risen with healing in His wings.
Mild He lays His glory by,
Born that man no more may die,
Born to raise the sons of earth,
Born to give them second birth.

'T was the night before Christmas,

when all through the house

Not a creature was stirring,

not even a mouse . . .

PART 25

BY MORLEY CALLAGHAN

AFTER MIDNIGHT ON **C**HRISTMAS **E**VE hundreds of people prayed at the crib of the Infant Jesus which was to the right of the altar under the evergreen-tree branches in St. Malachi's church. That night there had been a heavy fall of wet snow, and there was a muddy path up to the crib. Both Sylvanus O'Meara, the old caretaker who had helped to prepare the crib, and Father Gorman, the stout, red-faced, excitable parish priest, had agreed it was the most lifelike tableau of the Child Jesus in a corner of the stable at Bethlehem they had ever had in the church.

But early on Christmas morning Father Gorman came running to see O'Meara, the blood all drained out of his face and his hands pumping up and down at his sides and he shouted, "A terrible thing has happened. Where is the Infant Jesus? The crib's empty."

O'Meara, who was a devout, innocent, wondering old man, who prayed a lot and always felt very close to God in the church, was bewildered and he whispered, "Who could have taken it? Taken it where?"

"Take a look in the crib yourself, man, if you don't believe me," the priest said, and he grabbed the caretaker by the arm, marched him into the church and over to the crib and showed him that the figure of the Infant Jesus was gone.

"Someone took it, of course. It didn't fly away. But who took it, that's the question?" the priest said.

"When was the last time you saw it?"

A VERY MERRY CHRISTMAS

"I know it was here last night," O'Meara said, "because after the midnight mass when everybody else had gone home I saw Mrs. Farrel and her little boy kneeling up here, and when they stood up I wished them a merry Christmas. You don't think she'd touch it, do you?"

"What nonsense, O'Meara. There's not a finer woman in the parish. I'm going over to her house for dinner tonight."

"I noticed that she wanted to go home, but the little boy wanted to stay there and keep praying by the crib; but after they went home I said a few prayers myself and the Infant Jesus was still there."

Grabbing O'Meara by the arm the priest whispered excitedly, "It must be the work of communists or atheists." There was a sudden rush of blood to his face. "This isn't the first time they've struck at us," he said.

"What would communists want with the figure of the Infant Jesus?" O'Meara asked innocently. "They wouldn't want to have it to be reminded that God was with them. I didn't think

they could bear to have Him with them."

"They'd take it to mock us, of course, and to desecrate the church. O'Meara, you don't seem to know much about the times we live in. Why did they set fire to the church?"

O'Meara said nothing because he was very loyal and he didn't like to remind the priest that the little fire they had in the church a few months ago was caused by a cigarette butt the priest had left in his pocket when he was changing into his vestments, so he was puzzled and silent for a while and then whispered, "Maybe someone really wanted to take God away, do you think so?"

"Take Him out of the church?"

"Yes. Take Him away."

"How could you take God out of the church, man? Don't be stupid."

"But maybe someone thought you could, don't you see?"

"O'Meara, you talk like an old idiot. Don't you realize you play right into the hands of the atheists saying such things? Do we believe an image is God? Do we worship idols? We do not. No more of that, then. If communists and atheists tried to burn

this church once, they'll not stop till they desecrate it. God help us, why is my church marked out for this?" He got terribly excited and rushed away shouting, "I'm going to phone the police."

It looked like the beginning of a terrible Christmas Day for the parish. The police came, and were puzzled, and talked to everybody. Newspapermen came. They took pictures of the church and of Father Gorman, who had just preached a sermon that startled the congregation because he grew very eloquent on the subject of vandal outrages to the house of God. Men and women stood outside the church in their best clothes and talked very gravely. Everybody wanted to know what the thief would do with the image of the Infant Jesus. They all were wounded, stirred and wondering. There certainly was going to be something worth talking about at a great many Christmas dinners in the neighbourhood.

But Sylvanus O'Meara went off by himself and was very sad. From time to time he went into the church and looked at the empty crib. He had all kinds of strange thoughts. He told himself that if someone really wanted to hurt God, then just wishing harm to Him really hurt Him, for what other way was there of hurting Him? Last night he had had the feeling that God was all around the crib, and now it felt as if God wasn't there at all. It wasn't just that the image of the Infant Jesus was gone, but someone had done violence to that spot and driven God away from it. He told himself that things could be done that would make God want to leave a place. It was very hard to know where God was. Of course, He would always be in the church, but where had that part of Him that had seemed to be all around the crib gone?

It wasn't a question he could ask the little groups of astounded parishioners who stood on the sidewalk outside the church, because they felt like wagging their fingers and puffing their cheeks out and talking about what was happening to God in Mexico and Spain.

But when they had all gone home to eat their Christmas dinners, O'Meara, himself, began to feel a little hungry. He went out and stood in front of the church and was feeling thankful that there was so much snow for the children on Christmas Day when he saw that splendid and prominent woman, Mrs. Farrel, coming along the street with her little boy. On Mrs. Farrel's face there was a grim and desperate expression and she was taking such long fierce strides that the five-year-old boy, whose hand she held so tight, could hardly keep up with her and pull his big red sleigh. Sometimes the little boy tried to lean back and was a dead weight and then she pulled his feet off the ground while he whimpered, "Oh, gee, oh, gee, let me go." His red snowsuit was all covered with snow as if he had been rolling on the road.

"Merry Christmas, Mrs. Farrel," O'Meara said. And he called to the boy, "Not happy on Christmas day? What's the matter, son?"

"Merry Christmas, indeed, Mr. O'Meara," the woman snapped to him. She was not accustomed to paying much attention to the caretaker, a curt nod was all she ever gave him, and now she was far too angry and mortified to bother with him. "Where's Father Gorman?" she demanded.

"Still at the police station, I think."

"At the police station! God help us, did you hear that, Jimmie?" she said, and she gave such a sharp tug at the boy's arm that she spun him around in the snow behind her skirts where he cowered, watching O'Meara with a curiously steady pair of fine blue eyes. He wiped away a mat of hair from his forehead as he watched and waited. "Oh, Lord, this is terrible," Mrs. Farrel said. "What will I do?"

"What's the matter, Mrs. Farrel?"

"I didn't do anything," the child said. "I was coming back here. Honest I was, mister."

"Mr. O'Meara," the woman began, as if coming down from a great height to the level of an unimportant and simple-minded old man, "maybe you could do something for us. Look on the sleigh."

O'Meara saw that an old coat was wrapped around something on the sleigh, and stooping to lift it, he saw the figure of the Infant Jesus there. He was so delighted he only looked up at Mrs. Farrel and shook his head in wonder and said, "It's back and nobody harmed it at all."

"I'm ashamed, I'm terribly ashamed, Mr. O'Meara. You don't know how mortified I am," she said, "but the child really didn't know what he was doing. It's a disgrace to us, I know. It's my fault that I haven't trained him better, though God knows I've tried to drum respect for the church into him." She gave such a jerk at the child's hand he slid on his knee in the snow keeping his eyes on O'Meara.

Still unbelieving, O'Meara asked, "You mean he really took it from the church?"

"He did, he really did."

"Fancy that. Why, child, that was a terrible thing to do," O'Meara said. "Whatever got into you?" Completely mystified he turned to Mrs. Farrel, but he was so relieved to have the figure of the Infant Jesus back without there having been any great scandal that he couldn't help putting his hand gently on the child's head.

"It's all right, and you don't need to say anything," the child

said, pulling away angrily from his mother, and yet he never took his eyes off O'Meara, as if he felt there was some bond between them. Then he looked down at his mitts, fumbled with them and looked up steadily and said, "It's all right, isn't it, mister?"

"It was early this morning, right after he got up, almost the first thing he must have done on Christmas Day," Mrs. Farrel said. "He must have walked right in and picked it up and taken it out to the street."

"But what got into him?"

"He makes no sense about it. He says he had to do it."

"And so I did, 'cause it was a promise," the child said. "I promised last night, I promised God that if He would make Mother bring me a big red sleigh for Christmas I would give Him the first ride on it."

"Don't think I've taught the child foolish things," Mrs. Farrel said. "I'm sure he meant no harm. He didn't understand at all what he was doing."

Men and women stood outside the church in their best clothes and talked very gravely. Everybody wanted to know what the thief would do with the image of the Infant Jesus. They all were wounded, stirred and wondering

"Yes, I did," the child said stubbornly.

"Shut up, child," she said, shaking him.

O'Meara knelt down till his eyes were on a level with the child's and they looked at each other till they felt close together and he said, "But why did you want to do that for God?"

"'Cause it's a swell sleigh, and I thought God would like it."

Mrs. Farrel, fussing and red-faced, said, "Don't you worry. I'll see he's punished by having the sleigh taken away from him."

But O'Meara, who had picked up the figure of the Infant Jesus, was staring down at the red sleigh; and suddenly he had a feeling of great joy, of the illumination of strange good tidings, a feeling that this might be the most marvellous Christmas Day in the whole history of the city, for God must surely have been with the child, with him on a joyous, carefree holiday sleigh ride, as he ran along those streets and pulled the sleigh. And O'Meara turned to Mrs. Farrel, his face bright with joy, and said, commandingly, with a look in his eyes that awed her, "Don't you dare say a word to him, and don't you dare touch that sleigh, do you hear? I think God did like it."

PART 26

WE

➤ *A Christmas gathering at our Toronto house: friends, neighbours and relatives come and go, each of them leaving behind a Yuletide legacy of sincere good wishes*

THE SCARCITY OF FODDER IN WINTER MADE THE SLAUGHTER OF FARM ANIMALS NECESSARY AROUND AND ABOUT THE FIRST OF NOVEMBER (ALL SAINTS' DAY, THE "MORNING-AFTER" OF ALL HALLOWS EVE). ANGLO-SAXONS CONSIDERED THE

FEAST

wild boar's head a great succulent treat, stuck an apple or orange in its mouth, put sprigs of rosemary between its ears and made it the centrepiece of the Christmas feast. The wild boar became extinct in England in the sixteenth century, so a domestic pig was substituted. In Sweden the custom is still remembered with *lussekatter*, rolls often baked in the shape of the snouts of Yule boars.

With the disappearance of the wild boar, peacock became the new centrepiece in the great halls of the nobly born. The skin was stripped off with all the feathers still clinging to it, then the carcass was roasted, stuffed with spices and herbs. When it was half-cooled, the skin was put back on and sewn up. For decoration, the feathers were sometimes gilded and so was the beak, a dish fit for a king.

In non-noble homes, goose became the popular Christmas dish. Turkeys came in the latter part of the sixteenth century, after Spain conquered the Aztecs of Mexico, but the turkey didn't replace the goose in popularity until sometime in the nineteenth century.

Christmas is the time that I overdose on eggnog, especially now that it's made with two per cent milk. Its English ancestor is syllabub: wine, spices and creamed milk. Sounds curdling to me. Rum or brandy replaced the wine in North America. And Scandinavians drink something called, in Swedish, *glögg*. The English also drank something at Christmas called lamb's-wool, which is really mulled beer with apples floating in it. Wassail bowls, which were passed from lip to lip like a peace pipe, originally had pieces of toast floating in them, and that's where the idea of toasting came from. The empty bowl was then used for begging by the mummers.

Everybody at Christmas seems to eat more . . . if they can get it. A survey of the inhabitants of the Third World indicated that their fondest wish at this time of year is to have a piece of

meat to eat. Our ancestors who had the means really gorged themselves. They would start with a whole capon and move on to a salmon or a haunch of venison with kilderkins of mustard (whatever they are), then on to the game birds, including peacock, swan, heron, bustard, teal, mallard, pigeon and bittern. This was followed by the sweet stuff: custards and pancakes and plum puddings and apple pies, plus hogsheads of a honey wine called mead to wash it all down.

The Christmas pudding started out very simply as corn or wheat flour boiled in milk with a little sugar and spice, usually cinnamon. It was often given on Christmas Eve or Christmas morning as a fasting dish to tide you over until the big feast. But eggs were added and lumps of meat, and it was served on Christmas Day as a kind of shepherd's porridge or skinless haggis. I'm not sure how it lost its meaty taste and went all vegetarian and fruity. It's supposed to be made during the first week of Advent, and every member of the family should have a hand in stirring it.

In the sweets department, the Scots had a thick syrup called sowens, which they ate in their beds before arising on Christmas Day. Sounds a bit messy.

Originally mince pies had an oblong shape, like a coffin or a manger, and often a doll made of dough representing the baby Jesus was placed in it. The Puritans soon put a stop to that. Mince pies had a lot more meat in them when they started — mutton and ox tongue were important ingredients, as were pheasant and partridge. There was a pie served in a noble house in the Middle Ages that was three metres across and contained four wild ducks, four geese, four partridges, six snipes, seven blackbirds, six pigeons, two rabbits, two woodcocks, two neats' tongues, two curlews, seventy litres of flour and nine kilograms of butter. It weighed more than seventy-five kilograms. Anybody for seconds?

PART 27

CATHERINE'S
CHRISTMAS
COOKBOOK

C HRISTMAS STARTS FOR ME IN EARLY
September, when everything in the garden
is at its peak. This is the time for pickling
the bounty of green tomatoes into chowchow and
turning the juicy, ripened reds into chili sauce.
Donald, on his bicycle, claims he can smell my kitchen
a mile away.

October is the time to do the jars of mincemeat that
will provide the fillings for all those tarts, turnovers
and pies. In early November, I bake both the light and
dark Christmas cakes; cakes, like humans, have to sit
as they age. The light fruitcakes seem to be more
popular these past few Christmases; the dark ones
take more time to age, for the rich flavours to meld
together. When my sister, Patrician Anne, and I make
the fruitcakes in my country kitchen, we use a
roasting pan that can hold a fifteen-kilogram bird to
mix the batter. We make such a large quantity because
most of the cakes are given away as gifts, or they
go into food baskets containing each recipient's
personal favourites.

December is for baking cookies and making many of
the other dishes in this section. I love all the special
foods of this season and take pleasure in their
preparation, especially in their heavenly aromas.
Christmas is a time of tradition, from my mother's old
recipes to the dishes I've collected from family and
friends over the years. They have become my
tradition. I'm sure our daughter, Kelley, will do the
same thing when she starts her own family Christmas.

*Christmas dinner at our
country house near Barrie,
Ontario, might include two roast
ducks with stuffing and, left, sweet
potato supreme garnished with pecan
(recipes for both are included in this s
and salads depending on guests and a*

ves

on). I vary other vegetables

ability of ingredients and time

CATHERINE'S
Cranberry Bread

1	orange	1
	Orange rind, grated	
	Boiling water	
2 tbsp	butter	25 mL
1 cup	granulated sugar	250 mL
1	egg	1
1 cup	cranberries, chopped	250 mL
1/2 cup	walnuts, chopped	125 mL
2 cups	flour	500 mL
1/2 tsp	salt	2 mL
1/2 tsp	baking soda	2 mL

Squeeze the juice from the orange and add enough boiling water to make 3/4 cup (175 mL) of liquid. Add the grated orange rind. Add the 2 tbsp (25 mL) butter and stir until melted. In another bowl, beat together the egg and sugar. Stir into the orange mixture. Add the cranberries and walnuts. Sift together the flour, salt and baking soda. Stir into the wet ingredients. Spoon into a buttered, floured 9-inch (23 cm) loaf pan. Bake at 325°F (160°C) for one hour. The loaf freezes beautifully.

CHRISTMAS
Roast Duck Gourmet

I made this only once for Christmas, but I've served it at several dinner parties.

1 lb	raisin bread, sliced and toasted	500 g
1 1/2 cups	celery, chopped	375 mL
2	orange sections, chopped	2
2 1/2 tbsp	orange rind, grated	30 mL
1 tsp	salt	5 mL
1/4 tsp	dried thyme, crushed	1 mL
2 cups	orange juice	500 mL
2 tsp	soya sauce	10 mL
2 tbsp	flour	25 mL
1 cup	water	250 mL
2 tbsp	butter	25 mL

Chunks of day-old bread, enough to fill cavity of duck

Orange slices as garnish

U krainian Canadians celebrate Christmas on January 7. Their Christmas feast includes borscht, jellied stuffed fish, stuffed cabbage, figs and honey cake

Remove crusts from toasted raisin bread and cut into 1/2-inch (1 cm) cubes. Combine the raisin bread, celery, orange sections, 1 tsp (5 mL) orange rind, salt and thyme and mix lightly. Set aside. Stuff the duck with the day-old bread. Bake *covered* at 350°F (180°C) for one hour then remove bread and drain fat. Now stuff the duck with the prepared stuffing and roast *uncovered* at 425°F (220°C) for 15 minutes. Drain excess fat. Combine the remaining orange rind and 1 cup (250 mL) orange juice. Spoon half the mixture over duck. Bake *covered* in a 325°F (160°C) oven for 1 1/2 hours. Baste every half hour with remaining mixture. Add water to keep moist. Remove duck to heated platter. To make the gravy, add 1 cup (250 mL) orange juice and soya sauce to drippings in pan. Blend the flour, water and butter and add to pan. Cook, stirring, till thick. Garnish with orange slices.

NAN DEAR'S
(NOW FAMOUS)
Superlative Pâté

1 lb	chicken livers	500 g
1	medium onion, chopped	1
1/2 cup + 2 tbsp	butter	125 mL + 25 mL
1	large garlic glove, crushed	1
1/4 tsp	dried thyme	1 mL
1/8 tsp	nutmeg	0.5 mL
1 tsp	dried basil*	5 mL
3 tbsp	cream	50 mL
3 tbsp	brandy	50 mL
1 1 3/4-oz can	anchovy fillets	1 50 g can

Sauté the chicken livers and onions in 2 tbsp (25 mL) butter till cooked. In a small saucepan, melt the remaining butter and add the herbs and spices, cream and brandy. Purée the chicken livers and onions to the desired consistency, slowly adding the butter mixture and the anchovies, undrained. Chill overnight before serving. The pâté freezes beautifully; simply thaw to room temperature before serving. Serves eight to 10 as an appetizer. Note: do not make this the day you plan to serve it because it won't have time to set properly.
*If possible, I use fresh basil, about one-third of a bunch.

Sweet Potato Supreme

4	medium-size sweet potatoes	4
2 tbsp	cream or milk	25 mL
1/2 cup + 2 tbsp	butter	125 mL + 25 mL
	Scant teaspoon salt	
1/4 tsp	paprika	1 mL
1/2 cup	brown sugar, firmly packed	125 mL
1 cup	pecan halves	250 mL

Cook the sweet potatoes and mash well (they should yield about 2 cups [500 mL]). Melt the 2 tbsp (25 mL) butter and mix together with the sweet potatoes, cream or milk, salt and paprika. Spread the mixture in a greased casserole dish. Place in a 350°F (180°C) oven. Heat the brown sugar and 1/2 cup (125 mL) butter slowly, stirring constantly, until the butter is barely melted. (Important: do *not* cook after the butter has melted or the topping will harden.) Drizzle the brown sugar mixture over the sweet potato casserole as it is cooking. When the casserole is bubbling hot, remove from the oven and garnish with the pecan halves. Serves six.

Aunt Lillian's Tourtière

I serve this after midnight mass on Christmas Eve. Makes two pies

	Pastry for two double-crust 9-inch (23 cm) pies	
1 lb	ground beef	500 g
1 lb	ground pork	500 g
1	small onion, chopped	1
1	clove garlic	1
1 tsp	each ground cloves, cinnamon	5 mL
	and salt	
1/4 tsp	pepper	1 mL
1/2 cup	boiling water	125 mL

Put the meat, onion, garlic and spices in a large, heavy frying pan. Add the boiling water and cook slowly until the meat loses its pink colour, stirring constantly. Spread meat in the pastry-lined pie plates and top with the crusts. Seal the edges and cut slits in the top of each crust. Bake at 450°F (230°C) for 30 minutes. Serve piping hot. (I find these pies are even more flavourful when reheated.)

Nana Kinnon's
White Fruitcake

1 lb	*butter*	*500 g*
2 cups	*granulated sugar*	*500 mL*
8	*eggs*	*8*
	Juice of one lemon	
	Grated rind from one lemon	
4 cups	*all-purpose flour*	*1 L*
2 tsp	*baking powder*	*10 mL*
1 tsp	*salt*	*5 mL*
1½ lb	*white raisins*	*750 g*
1 lb	*candied red cherries*	*500 g*
1 lb	*candied green cherries*	*500 g*
½ lb	*blanched almonds (optional)**	*250 g*
½ lb	*mixed candied peel, cut*	*250 g*
½ lb	*citron, cut*	*250 g*
½ lb	*candied pineapple rings*	*250 g*

Dust the fruit with 1 cup (250 mL) of the flour. Cream together the butter and sugar. Add the eggs and the lemon juice and rind. Combine the remaining 3 cups (750 mL) of flour with the baking powder and salt, add to the butter mixture and mix well. Add the prepared fruit. Put in pans that have been greased and lined with one layer of brown paper and one layer of waxed paper. Bake in a 300°F (150°C) oven for three hours, reducing the temperature to 275°F (140°C) after the first hour to prevent the cakes from becoming brown. Yields three fruitcakes when baked in the old-fashioned round fruitcake pans — one 8-inch (20 cm), one 9-inch (23 cm), one 10-inch (25 cm).

*I have *never* used almonds in Nana Kinnon's white fruitcake recipe because they may not be fresh when they're purchased, which will ruin the cake *and* all that work. Stale almonds once tainted Aunt Lillian's fruitcake and I've never used them since.

MY MOTHER'S
Honey Bars

BOTTOM

1/2 cup	butter	125 mL
1/2 cup	granulated sugar	125 mL
2	egg yolks, slightly beaten	2
2 cups	pastry flour	500 mL
2 cups	walnuts, chopped	500 mL
1 cup	unsweetened coconut	250 mL

FILLING

2	egg whites	2
2 cups	brown sugar	500 mL
1/2 tsp	vanilla	2 mL

Walnut halves for garnish

MY MOTHER'S **POUND CAKE**

Cream the butter and sugar together, then add the egg yolks. Mix in the flour until it reaches a mealy consistency. Press into the bottom of a 9-inch (23 cm) square pan. Sprinkle the walnuts and coconut over the bottom layer. For the filling, beat the egg whites till stiff, then gradually fold in the brown sugar and vanilla. Spread on top. Garnish with the walnut halves, one per square. Bake at 325°F (160°C) for 45 minutes. Cut into squares when still slightly warm.

MY MOTHER'S
Pound Cake

1 cup	soft butter	250 mL
2³/4 cups	granulated sugar	675 mL
6	eggs	6
3 cups	flour	750 mL
1/2 tsp	salt	2 mL
1 cup	sour cream	250 mL
1 tsp	vanilla	5 mL
1 tsp	lemon extract	5 mL

A little lemon peel, if desired

Icing sugar

Cream the butter and sugar together and beat until light. Add the eggs, one at a time, and beat. Add the dry ingredients, alternating with the sour cream. Add the flavouring. Bake in a 10-inch (25 cm) springform pan at 350°F (180°C), testing after one hour. Dust with icing sugar. Makes one *very moist* pound cake.

HELEN McKINNON'S
Molasses Kisses

1 cup	molasses	250 mL
3 cups	granulated sugar	750 mL
1 cup	boiling water	250 mL
3 tbsp	vinegar	45 mL
1/2 tsp	cream of tartar	2 mL
1/4 tsp	baking soda	1 mL
1/2 cup	melted butter	125 mL
2 tsp	vanilla	10 mL

Heat the molasses, sugar, water and vinegar in a saucepan. When it comes to a boil, add the cream of tartar and boil until the mixture becomes brittle when added to cold water (265°F [130°C]). Stir constantly in the last stage of cooking. When it is done, add the baking soda and butter. Stir well. Remove from the heat and add the vanilla. Cool and pull like molasses taffy until porous; be sure to keep your hands well buttered. Twist into a rope and cut into small pieces with buttered scissors. Let them cool on wax paper. Makes about 1¹/2 pounds (750 g).

F rench Canadians celebrate on December 24 following the messe de minuit *(midnight mass) with the* réveillon de Noël. *After the meal, which is likely to include* tourtière *and a* bûche de Noël, *dancing and games continue until sunrise*

MY MOTHER'S
Green Tomato Mincemeat

For more than a hundred years in England, mince pies were the centre of theological discussion, and puritanical clergymen preached to their flocks to abstain from this unholy fare. But by the time settlers arrived in the Maritimes, the mince pie had been cleansed of all sin and was able to take a place of honour in the pie cupboard. I've only made mincemeat from scratch a few times, but it's a wonderful feeling of satisfaction and truly makes terrific pies, tarts and turnovers. This is a very old recipe.

3 lb	green tomatoes	1.5 kg
1 cup	ground suet	250 mL
1 cup	vinegar	250 mL
2 lb	raisins	1 kg
3 lb	apples, chopped	1.5 kg
4 lb	brown sugar	2 kg
2 tbsp	salt	25 mL
2 tsp	cloves	10 mL
1 tsp	ginger	5 mL
2 tsp	cinnamon	10 mL
1 tsp	nutmeg	5 mL

Rind from one orange and one lemon

Chop the tomatoes or put them through a food chopper. Allow them to drain, then cover with cold water. Bring the tomatoes to a boil and let them boil for five minutes. Drain well, then add the other ingredients. Cook slowly for 30 to 45 minutes (until thick). (I find it can take longer.) Pack in sterilized jars and seal with wax. Makes about four quarts (4 L).

AUNT JEANNE'S
Mincemeat Turnovers

1 lb	butter, chilled	500 g
4 cups	all-purpose flour	1 L
1 cup	sour cream	250 mL
1½ cups	mincemeat	375 mL

Cut the butter into chunks with a pastry blender, then cut it into the flour until it's like coarse meal. Add the sour cream and stir until just blended. The dough will be quite soft. Shape into a ball, wrap in waxed paper and chill at least two hours. Divide the dough in half (keeping the other portion chilled) and roll out to a thickness of ½ inch (1 cm). Cut into 3-inch (7.5 cm) squares or rounds. Put 1 tsp

(5 mL) mincemeat in the centre of each and fold over to the opposite corner. Pinch with a fork and seal well. Place turnovers on a greased baking sheet and bake at 375°F (190°C) for 15 to 20 minutes, or till nearly brown. Cool them slightly on the pan then remove to racks. The turnovers can be frozen; simply reheat three to five minutes in a 375°F (190°C) preheated oven. Makes 50 to 60 turnovers.

Viennese Crescents

1 cup	butter	250 mL
¼ cup	granulated sugar	50 mL
1¾ cups	flour	425 mL
1 cup	blanched almonds, ground	250 mL
1 tsp	vanilla	5 mL
	Icing sugar	

Mix together all the ingredients, except the icing sugar, in the order given. Cream and shape into crescents. Arrange on a buttered cookie sheet. Bake at 300°F (150°C) for 35 minutes. Roll the crescents in the icing sugar. Let them cool, then roll in sugar again. Store in an airtight cookie tin. Makes about three dozen.

NANA KINNON'S
Dark Irish Fruitcake

1 cup	salt pork, diced	250 mL
1 cup	boiling water	250 mL
2 tsp	baking soda	10 mL
1 cup	molasses	250 mL
1 cup	brown sugar	250 mL
2	eggs, separated	2
1 tsp	ground cloves	5 mL
2 tsp	cinnamon	10 mL
1 tsp	each nutmeg, mace and allspice	5 mL
4 cups	all-purpose flour, sifted	1 L
1 lb	seedless raisins	500 g
1 lb	currants	500 g
1 lb	mixed candied peel, cut	500 g
½ lb	mixed candied fruit	250 g
½ lb	candied red and green cherries	250 g
1½ tsp	lemon extract	7 mL
1 tsp	lemon rind, grated	5 mL

Dice the salt pork in a food chopper, removing any bits of lean meat. Cover with the boiling water and let stand five minutes, until cool. Add the baking soda, molasses and sugar, stirring until dissolved. Add the well-beaten egg yolks. In a separate bowl, combine the fruit and 1 cup (250 mL) sifted flour. Mix well. Add the fruit mixture and the remaining flour. Add spices and flavouring, then fold in the stiffly beaten egg whites. Pour into three 8-inch (20 cm) round or square pans, lined with oiled and floured brown paper. Cover the fruitcakes with tin foil and bind tightly with string. Place on a rack in a large pot, filled with enough water to come halfway up the pan. Cover and steam one hour, then bake in a 300°F (150°C) oven for two hours. Store two weeks before serving. Yields six pounds (3 kg) fruitcake.

TISTIE'S
Chocolate Cake

5 *tbsp*	cocoa	**75** *mL*
2 *cups*	granulated sugar	**500** *mL*
1/2 *cup*	butter	**125** *mL*
1 *cup*	boiling water	**250** *mL*
2	eggs	**2**
1/2 *cup*	sour milk*	**125** *mL*
2 *tbsp*	baking soda	**25** *mL*
1 *tsp*	vanilla	**5** *mL*
1 *tsp*	salt	**5** *mL*
2 *cups*	flour	**500** *mL*

Combine the cocoa, sugar, butter and boiling water. Add the eggs, sour milk, baking soda, vanilla, salt and flour. Mix well. The batter is very thin. Pour into a 12-inch (30 cm) cast-iron frying pan and bake at 350°F (180°C) for one hour. (The cake does not rise very much.) *To sour, add 1 tsp (5 mL) vinegar to the milk.

MY MOTHER'S
Shortbread
(THE BEST)

1 1/2 *cups*	cornstarch	**375** *mL*
1/2 *tsp*	salt	**2** *mL*
1 *cup*	icing sugar	**250** *mL*
2 1/2 *cups*	flour	**625** *mL*
1 *lb*	butter, salted	**500** *g*

Sift all the dry ingredients well. Work the butter into the mixture using your hands (keep them cold with ice water so the butter won't melt). Roll out the dough to 1/4 inch (5 mm) thick and cut into shapes. Place on a greased cookie sheet and bake at 330°F (165°C) for 10 minutes, *without opening the oven door*. They will burn easily. Makes approximately 50 shortbread cookies.

PATRICIAN ANNE'S
(MY SISTER'S)
Angel Lemon Pie

1	9-inch (23 cm) pie shell, baked	**1**
	FILLING	
4	egg yolks	**4**
3/4 *cup*	granulated sugar	**175** *mL*
1/4 *cup*	lemon juice	**50** *mL*
1 *tbsp*	butter	**15** *mL*
2	egg whites	**2**

MERINGUE

2	egg whites	2
4 tbsp	granulated sugar	**60** mL
1 tsp	lemon juice	**5** mL

To make the lemon filling, cream together the egg yolks and sugar. Pour this mixture into a double boiler and add the lemon juice. Cook in the double boiler until stiffened, stirring frequently. This procedure should take about 10 minutes. Add the butter, then remove from the heat. Beat the egg whites until stiff, then fold them into the lemon mixture. Pour the filling into the pie shell. To make the meringue, beat the egg whites till frothy. Continue beating while gradually adding the sugar until the egg holds its shape in peaks when the beaters are lifted. Fold in the lemon juice. Spread the meringue over the filling. Brown the pie in a 325°F (160°C) oven for 15 minutes. The recipe makes one pie.

PATRICIAN ANNE'S **ANGEL LEMON PIE**

*T*he Acadians of New Brunswick celebrate Christmas Eve with a late-night meal of meat pie and poutine râpée

AUNT LILLIAN'S
Dream Relish

1 quart	cucumbers, chopped	*1 L*
1 quart	onions, chopped	*1 L*
2	bunches celery, chopped	*2*
1	red hot pepper, chopped	*1*
2	sweet red peppers, chopped	*2*
3	sweet green peppers, chopped	*3*
3 tbsp	salt	*50 mL*
1¼ quarts	vinegar	*1.25 L*
2 tbsp	mustard seeds	*25 mL*
6 cups	granulated sugar	*1.5 L*
¾ cup	flour	*200 mL*
4 tbsp	turmeric	*60 mL*
½ cup	cold water	*125 mL*

Sprinkle the salt on the vegetables and let stand overnight. Rinse the mixture then put it through a very fine food chopper. Add the vinegar, mustard seeds and sugar and bring to a boil. Boil slowly and stir until vegetables are clear. In another pot mix together the flour, turmeric and cold water; boil five minutes (add some of the hot mixture so it won't go lumpy). You may need to add a little more water. Pour the flour mixture into the vegetable mixture and stir well. Put the relish in sterilized jars. Makes about nine pints (4.5 L).

MARY ELLEN'S
Cabbage Pickle

5 lb	cabbage, finely chopped	2.5 kg
6	medium onions, finely chopped	6
2	green peppers, finely chopped	2
2	red peppers, finely chopped	2
1/2 cup	pickling salt	125 mL
3/4 cup	mustard seeds	175 mL
2 tbsp	celery seeds	25 mL
4 cups	granulated sugar	1 L
	Vinegar	

Mix the vegetables in a bowl, add the salt, stir well and let stand 24 hours. Rinse and drain well. Add the mustard seeds, celery seeds and sugar and mix well. Add enough vinegar to cover. Pack in sterilized jars. Store in a cool place. Yields about nine pints (4.5 L).

Champagne Jelly

2 cups	sparkling wine or champagne	500 mL
3 cups	granulated sugar	750 mL
1/2 bottle	Certo (liquid pectin)	1/2 bottle

Mix the wine and sugar in a double boiler. Place over rapidly boiling water and stir until the sugar dissolves (about two minutes). Remove from the heat and stir in Certo. Pour quickly into sterilized jars and cover with wax. Yields about four medium-size mason jars.

NANA KINNON'S
Chowchow

1 quart	green tomatoes	1 L
6	onions	6
2	red or green peppers	2
3 tbsp	pickling salt	50 mL
2 quarts	cider vinegar	2 L
4 tbsp	mustard seeds	60 mL
3 tbsp	turmeric	50 mL
1 tbsp	each allspice, pepper and cloves	15 mL
	Gauze bag of pickling spices	

Chop the vegetables into small pieces or use a food processor. Cover with cold water and sprinkle with the salt. Let stand overnight. Rinse and drain well. Combine vinegar, mustard seeds, turmeric, allspice, pepper and cloves and bring to the boil. Pour over the vegetables and cook until tender with the pickling spices hanging in the pot. Stir often. Put in sterilized jars. Makes approximately eight pints (4 L).

Bread & Butter Pickles

4 quarts	cucumber, sliced	4 L
6	medium onions, sliced	6
1	green pepper	1
1	red pepper	1
Pinch	garlic salt	Pinch
1/3 cup	coarse pickling salt	75 mL
5 cups	granulated sugar	1.25 L
3 cups	distilled white vinegar	750 mL
1 1/2 tsp	each turmeric and celery seeds	7 mL
2 tbsp	mustard seeds	25 mL

Use medium-size, firm cucumbers. Wash well and slice thinly — *do not peel.* Prepare the onions. Wash the peppers, remove stems and seeds and cut into thin strips. Layer the vegetables in a large crock or bowl, sprinkle combined salts over each layer. Mix a tray of ice cubes through the vegetables and cover with another tray of ice cubes. Let stand three hours. Rinse and drain vegetables well. Combine the sugar, vinegar, turmeric, celery seeds and mustard seeds and pour over the drained pickles. Heat only to the boiling point — that's all the cooking required. Ladle into sterilized jars. For the best flavour, store the pickles one month before using. Yields about 10 pints (5 L).

Zucchini Pickle

2 lb	small zucchini, sliced	1 kg
2 lb	medium onions, thinly sliced	1 kg
1/4 cup	pickling salt	50 mL
2 cups	white vinegar	500 mL
1 cup	granulated sugar	250 mL
1/2 tsp	dry mustard	2 mL
1 tsp	celery seeds	5 mL
1 tsp	mustard seeds	5 mL
1 tsp	turmeric	5 mL

Place the onions and zucchini in a bowl and cover with water. Add the pickling salt and let stand for one hour, then drain and rinse. In a pot, combine the remaining ingredients and bring to the boil. Pour over the zucchini and onions. Let the mixture stand for one hour, then bring to the boil and cook for three minutes. Pack in sterilized jars and seal. Yields three pints (1.5 L).

Notes

PART 28

FOR THE KIDS

WHEN **I** STARTED RESEARCHING CHILDREN'S Christmas games, I realized that I had never played most of them. I have played a version of hoodman-blind and bobbing for apples, but never snapdragon, steal the white loaf, hot cockles and shoeing the wild mare. I found out this last one involves a hearty slap on the instep. Nuts and May sounds like a gathering game; I only knew it as a round game in kindergarten. Hot cockles is another whacking good game, where a player is blindfolded, then whacked on the hand until the whackee guesses who has done the deed and whether it was done out of lust or spite.

I think I have played puss in the corner, but not the way it's described as being played a couple of hundred years ago. It sounds like a hide-and-seek game, but originally it involved a lot of fierce kissing. Postman's knock and spin the bottle were the kissing games in which I got involved, sometimes emotionally. Spin the bottle was public kissing, as with mistletoe, and postman's knock, much more exciting, was done behind closed doors. Hunt the slipper is something I do almost every morning when I get up in the dark. Blindman's buff has a rather gruesome origin — it's said that the game was used on people who were actually blind, and the idea was to get them to trip over the furniture.

For me, Canadian Christmases conjure up the game of crokinole, when cousins with whom you had been playing in a

friendly manner at snap or old maid or Chinese checkers suddenly became deadly rivals. When I lived abroad in England or in New York or Los Angeles, I was amazed to find that no one had ever heard of crokinole. Perhaps that's because it's all our own. It was invented in southwestern Ontario more than a hundred years ago.

Newfoundland has games like spin the bottle and musical chairs, but it also has a few that are new to me. You, you, you is a game in which a bunch of men sit on chairs formed in a circle and each man has a woman on his lap, except for one man, who stands in the centre of the circle. His job is to point at one of the men and say, "You, you, you" before the seated man has time to shout one "You." If that happens, the two men change places, and this goes on until they all get tired of all that finger pointing and go on to something else.

Sir Roger must be a short form of the English country-dance Sir Roger de Coverley, but it sounds more like what used to happen at our high school dances when the music would stop and you would dance with the girl facing you. Newfoundland men sing about "catching a little fox," then grab the nearest woman and march her around the room. Tucker is where ladies and gents face each other in two straight lines and proceed to swing each other to the music of an accordion. The ring game involves more individual choice. One group forms a circle and marches clockwise around the room. Two or three people remain in the centre and everyone sings:

Sailing in the boat till the tide runs high (repeat three times)

Waiting for the pretty girls coming by and by;

Choose your partner now to-day (repeat three times)

For I don't care what the old folks say;

Since you can no longer stay,

Give her a kiss and send her away.

If she's not there to take your part,

Choose another with all your heart,

Down on this carpet you must kneel

 t as the grass grows in the field.

Kiss your true love, kiss her sweet

You may rise upon your feet.

The games I remember most vividly are the ones that my family made up all by itself. My father was always the master of the games, and my mother was his chief henchperson. They had a noisy card game called pig, which was a variant on the theme of old maid. It consisted of passing playing cards to the next person face down (the cards, not the person) and trying to gather groups of four so you would have fewer cards in your hand. The word *pass* was shouted at the top of the lungs every four or five seconds, which rattled both the younger and the older members of my extended family. My mother was the best player . . . she had a beatific smile on her face as she encouraged some poor dupe to think he or she was safe and continue shouting, "Pass" when everyone else was finished. If you were the last one left with cards in your hand three times in a row, you became a hog.

A game I assumed my father had made up, and which was the favourite of everyone in our family, was called the drawing game. The assembled company was divided up into two teams, with the exception of my father, who sat between them. Each team had a card table, pencils and lots of scrap paper. Two players would approach my dad and he would print something on a card for them to draw. Usually both players would squeal in either horror or delight, rush to their tables and begin drawing Mae West or Big Ben or a giraffe. The decibel level was horrendous as the rest of the team shouted possible answers.

You probably know all about this game because it's now on network television, but at the time we thought it was our family's private playground. Recently Kelley, our twenty-one-year-old daughter, had a sophisticated dinner party. It was a very well behaved affair until about one o'clock in the morning when I was awakened by loud shrieks coming from the living room below. She had taught her friends the drawing game.

There were always practical jokes round our house at Christmas, usually purchased at a so-called magic store. A tin ink blot caused hypertension in the hostess when placed on a white tablecloth just before Christmas dinner. Rubber bulbs placed under dinner plates caused them to heave as if the weight of all that food was too much for them.

It wasn't long before I was seeking out that same joke store to buy plastic ice cubes with flies trapped inside, chewing gum that burned hot on your tongue and a hideously realistic bit of plastic excrement called Blame It on the Dog. But I once stooped lower than that. I remember getting my sister to put her fingers through the jamb of the front door of our house and after putting an egg in those fingers, I carefully placed my father's best hat on the floor directly below the egg and left her to her own devices.

Each year, Canadians exchange an estimated 150 million Christmas cards

Santa's Reindeer

Rudolph the Red-Nosed Reindeer is wrapping presents for Santa's other reindeer. What are the eight different names Rudolph has to write on the presents?

Dasher, Dancer, Prancer, Vixen, Comet, Cupid, Donder, Blitzen

Hidden Words

Many people travel home for Christmas. How many different words can you make from the letters in the word **Travel?** (Hint: there are at least ten different words.)

Rat, tar, real, read, ale, vat, let, rave, ear, art, rate, vale, tear, late

Christmas Decorations

(The kind you can eat)

Adults should help with this simple recipe for cookies.
1 cup (250 mL) butter (melt first)
½ cup (125 mL) granulated sugar
½ cup (125 mL) brown sugar
one egg
1 tsp (5 mL) vanilla
2 cups (500 mL) all-purpose flour
1 tsp (5 mL) baking soda
1 tsp (5 mL) cream of tartar

In separate bowls, mix the dry ingredients together and the liquid ingredients together. Gradually add the dry mixture to the liquid mixture, blending thoroughly. Let the batter stand three to four hours or overnight. Roll out the batter and cut into shapes with cookie cutters. Near the top of each shape, poke a tiny hole with a toothpick. Bake at 350°F (180°C) for six or seven minutes, until golden brown. When cool, run a short piece of coloured string through each cookie and hang up on the tree. Of course, you can add colour or sparkles to the cookies before baking them if you wish.

Triangle Puzzle

Try this puzzle with ten Christmas ornaments: turn the triangle upside-down by moving only three ornaments.

(Answer on page 149)

Dumb Riddle

What did Mrs. Claus say to Santa after hearing the Christmas Eve weather forecast for Vancouver?

"I hope it doesn't rein, deer."

Santa's Christmas Route

Santa Claus is planning the route he'll take across Canada on Christmas Eve. He's decided that he'll visit the provinces and territories in alphabetical order. Can you arrange these places in the order in which Santa will be visiting?

Newfoundland, Ontario, Saskatchewan, Northwest Territories, British Columbia, Prince Edward Island, Alberta, New Brunswick, Manitoba, Nova Scotia, Yukon, Quebec

Alberta, British Columbia, Manitoba, New Brunswick, Newfoundland, Northwest Territories, Nova Scotia, Ontario, Prince Edward Island, Quebec, Saskatchewan, Yukon

Hidden Words

Everybody likes to build a snowman in the winter. How many different words can you make from the letters in **Snowman?** (Hint: there are at least ten different words.)

Man, woman, snow, mow, now, won, an, saw, sow, on, own, no, son, was, moan

FOUR SQUARES, TWO SQUARES

Arrange twelve identical Christmas candles in the design shown below. Can you remove two candles and leave only two squares? (A square has four sides of equal length.)

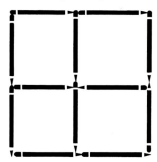

(ANSWER ON PAGE 149)

THE MEMORY GAME

On a large tray place a dozen or so objects — an ornament, a Christmas tree light, a candy, etcetera — and pass it around so the entire group can see. Putting the tray out of sight, ask each player in turn what was on it. The player who remembers the most objects gets to keep his or her choice. The game can be repeated until everything on the tray is gone.

LAST LETTER STARTS

(For two or more players)

Flip a coin to see who starts. The player who begins says a word that has to do with the Christmas season. The word "gift" would be a good one or even "Christmas." It's up to the next player to say another seasonal word that begins with the last letter of the word that was just said. If it was "gift," for example, the letter would be "t"; if it was "Christmas," the letter would be "s." And then the next player has to say a word that begins with the last letter of the word said by Player #2, and so on. If a player can't come up with a new word, he or she drops out. The last player who isn't stumped is the winner.

THE TWELVE MISTAKES OF CHRISTMAS

Find the twelve errors in this story: *(ANSWER ON PAGE 149)*
Santa Claus put on his green suit and hitched his cows to the sleigh. He was ready to deliver gifts to all the bad little boys and girls around the world.

"Ho, ho, hee!" he laughed, and his belly shook like a bowlful of peanut butter.

"Where are my helpers?" Santa wondered. "Where are those little leprechauns?"

Just then Santa's helpers came out from his workshop, their arms loaded down with presents and bright shiny toads. "Where should we put these, Santa?" they asked.

"Why, put them in the sleigh!" said Santa. "It's New Year's Eve and I've got many places to go tonight."

And so, with his long pink beard flowing behind him, and with Roger the Red-Nosed Reindeer leading the way, Santa and his sleigh flew away from his home at the South Pole.

And you could hear him exclaim as he drove out of sight, "Happy Christmas to all, and to all a good afternoon!"

CRAZY MIXED-UP TREE

Rearrange these letters to find a kind of tree that is commonly associated with Christmas. *(ANSWER ON PAGE 149)*

N E R E R V E G E

CHRISTMAS CARD CHALLENGE

Try to draw this Christmas card envelope using one continuous line — no retracing.

(ANSWER ON PAGE 149)

COOKIE TWINS

Only two of these Christmas tree cookies are exactly the same. Can you find the two that match?

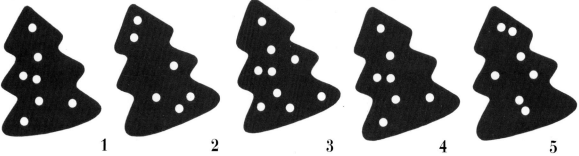

1   **2**   **3**   **4**   **5**

(ANSWER ON PAGE 149)

CHRISTMAS "LANTERNS" FOR THE TREE

Sheets of silver or gold paper are best here. Fold a sheet in half. With a pair of scissors, make a series of cuts in the side with the fold three-quarters of the way into the sheet. It should look like the illustration on the left.

Now, using glue or Scotch tape, fasten the unattached sides together and squeeze the sides to make the "lantern" open up. And then make a handle, attaching it to the top. You can now hang your lantern on the Christmas tree.

DELIVERING PRESENTS

This game depends on everyone's ability to spin out a story — and to make everybody else participate. Bring all players together in the same room. One person is selected to be the storyteller, spinning a tale about a trip in the family car delivering presents. Everyone else must choose to become a part of the car — a tire, a door, the windshield, a front fender. The storyteller writes down a list of these various car parts. As the story unfolds, each time a particular part is mentioned, the person matching the part must stand up and sit down again. Each time the word "car" is mentioned, everybody must stand up. Any player forgetting to stand up must pay a penalty — standing and sitting twice the next time around. The object for the storyteller is to spin out the tale as long as possible, making as many references to as many parts of the car as he or she can.

THE SNOWBALL GAME

This game must be played with an even number of people — six or eight, for example. First, take several sheets of the same coloured paper and cut out a number of circles — the "snowballs" for the game. Now, cut each of these circles into two pieces — not perfect halves, but, using jagged lines and curves, so that only the two parts of each snowball will fit together. Place all the parts in a hat or box and have all the players draw out a piece. Then, on the word "go," all the players scramble to find the matching part of their snowball. The two players who last put their snowball together must pay a predetermined penalty.

THE CANDY CANE GAME

The object of this game is to have someone guess a word that everyone hides by saying "candy cane" in its place. After you get all the players together, send whoever is It out of the room. One person left in the room is group leader. When everyone agrees on the word, the person who is It is invited back to the room. Then the group leader asks everyone except It a question that forces them to use the hidden word. For instance, if the hidden word was "cat," you might hear the following:

"John, what do you do when you get home from school?"
"Oh, I feed my candy cane."

"Emily, who is your favourite cartoon character?"
"Garfield the candy cane."

A LITTLE MAGIC

Trace Figure A and cut it out (please don't cut this page). Make one cut in Figure A and rearrange the pieces to form Figure B.

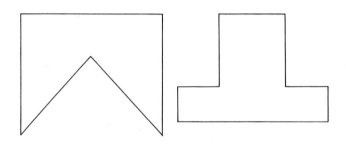

(ANSWER ON PAGE 149)

CHRISTMAS CHAINS

Using sheets of red and green paper, cut a series of strips about ten centimetres long and one or two centimetres wide. Use these pieces as loops to make your chain, alternating different colours. Fasten each piece together with Scotch tape or glue. You can make the chain as long as you wish.

TRIANGLE PUZZLE

FOUR SQUARES, TWO SQUARES

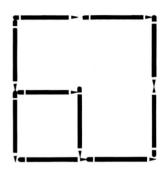

COOKIE TWINS

COOKIES 1 AND 4

A LITTLE MAGIC

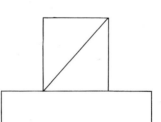

THE TWELVE MISTAKES OF CHRISTMAS

1. *Green* suit should be *red*; 2. *Cows* should be *reindeer*; 3. *Bad* should be *good*; 4. *Ho, ho, hee* should be *Ho, ho, ho*; 5. *Peanut butter* should be *jelly*; 6. *Leprechauns* should be *elves*; 7. *Toads* should be *toys*; 8. *New Year's Eve* should be *Christmas Eve*; 9. *Pink* beard should be *white*; 10. *Roger* should be *Rudolph*; 11. *South Pole* should be *North Pole*; 12. *Good afternoon* should be *good night*.

CRAZY MIXED-UP TREE

EVERGREEN

CHRISTMAS CARD CHALLENGE

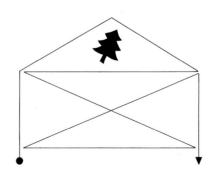

PART 29

CHRISTMAS DAY

T HE ONE THING CATHERINE insists on is that we spend part of Christmas morning listening to the Queen's message. In these days of pre-recording, it's sometimes hard to find it in the listings. We are accustomed to it about ten o'clock in the morning, but last year we had to settle for a re-run Christmas night.

`I remember still the Christmas speeches given by our current Queen's father during World War II. These were live radio broadcasts that contained a great deal of suspense, because all the subjects of King George VI knew he was a shy, reserved man who had a speech impediment. Sometimes there was an agonizing pause as he struggled to say the next word, and we were all with him in that struggle. This was at a time when we were not at all sure of the outcome of the war, and the Royal Family's bravery in staying in London during the nightly rain of bombs was a morale booster for us far-flung colonials.

We didn't find out till after the war what a

➤ *STARS EMBLAZE THE FAÇADE OF THE CHÂTEAU FRONTENAC HOTEL IN QUEBEC CITY; FOR CHILDREN, ABOVE, CHRISTMAS DAY IS FOR TRYING NEW TOYS*

morale booster his wife had been to him during those difficult-to-deliver Christmas messages. Canadians had a distinct image of a woman in powder blue waving and smiling beside our King because of the royal visit during the summer of 1939.

There is a funny story about an incident during that royal tour that the Queen Mother still loves to tell. At a Buckingham Palace garden party just before the Canadian tour was to begin, someone slipped a message into the Queen's hand as she stood in the receiving line. The message read, "The citizens of Swastika, Ontario, are loyal Canadian citizens. Please find time to greet them during your visit to Northern Ontario."

Since the main purpose of the 1939 royal visit was to prepare Canada to participate in the world war that loomed in the near future, the Queen decided that a town named after the insignia chosen by the Nazis deserved some attention. (Actually, the swastika comes from India, where it is a sign of peace. It's plastered all over Rudyard Kipling's books.) The royal equerry who had planned the tour shook his head and said, "Your Majesty, this would be impossible. We pass through this remote village at four o'clock in the morning on our way to Port Arthur and Fort William."

The Queen gave her most radiant smile and said, "Nevertheless, I want you to arrange a ten-minute stop to greet the citizens of Swastika." The royal command was obeyed and the tour arrangements were slightly shifted to take care of this request and accommodate the stop.

As the train trundled across the great Canadian Shield, the Queen was awakened by the porter at the ungodly hour of 3 a.m., and she in turn awakened the King, who was commanded to put on his uniform of admiral of the fleet and also a bit of tan makeup to take away the morning (morning? post-midnight surely!) pallor.

The royal train rolled into Swastika right on time, and the royal couple dutifully appeared on the little platform at the rear of the last railway car. They were greeted by a thick curtain of dense fog. But out of that fog came a tiny, muffled cheer some two hundred metres away. The Queen smiled with relief and asked the cheerers to approach.

A knot of about thirty people appeared out of the fog and gathered round the royal pair. There was a long moment of Canadian silence. The Queen was waiting for someone in authority to speak. Finally, out of embarrassment, she found it necessary to speak herself: "Is there a person among you who represents the town?"

A little man stepped forward. "Yes, Your Majesty. I am the mayor of Swastika."

The Queen paused. "Oh, I'm sorry I didn't recognize you. Don't you possess some insignia of your office, like a chain you wear around your neck?"

Back came the reply: "Yes, Your Majesty, but I only wear it on special occasions."

They say it's the Queen Mom's favourite story.

➤ MIDNIGHT MASS ON CHRISTMAS EVE AT NOTRE-DAME-DE-SEPT-DOULEURS CHURCH IN EDMUNDSTON, NEW BRUNSWICK; MARIE-PIER, BELOW, MIGHT SURPRISE SANTA

Recent Christmas music written by Canadians includes "Christmas Kaleidoscope," by Alfred Kunz (1985); "Christmas Fantasy," by Wolfgang Bottenberg (1986); and "Christmas Fanfare," by Nancy Telfer (1985)

PART 30

FINAL FEW WORDS

FOR SOME REASON **C**HRISTMAS ACTS LIKE A lightning rod for emotional tensions that lie hidden at other times of the year. Distress centres work overtime during the happy holidays. It seems to be a time of desperate, violent decisions; marriage breakups; disastrous fires with loss of life; even suicides. The rate of self-destruction jumps precipitously during the festive season.

The biological explanation is that such acts are caused by the release of a hormone in the pineal gland called melatonin; the body does this because of a lack of sunlight at this time of year, and seventy per cent of us are affected by it. Five per cent go into deep depression as they recall happier holiday times in their remote past. For many, Christmas can seem like an

artificial striving for happiness. As one urban transient said, "It's just another day to me, I'm not a kid anymore."

Newspapers record many tragic incidents in their editions on December 26. There is usually a Christmas orphan, a baby abandoned on some institutional doorstep. The unrecorded incidents can be just as sad. This time of year is especially hard for the lonely, the poor, the ill, the old, the imprisoned and the homeless. Add to that the unemployed, many of whom are having their first experience of being on welfare. For those who could formerly afford Christmas, the holiday season becomes especially traumatic for their self-esteem.

Organized groups like the Salvation Army, which dispense charity three hundred and sixty-five days of the year, give up

Λ *WE MUST STRIVE TO REMEMBER THOSE LESS FORTUNATE THAN US*

sense of being shut out is more vivid.

There are more than a few restaurants that open their doors to the homeless on Christmas Day, and there was the case recently of the homeless couple who were invited to spend Christmas Eve sleeping in the foyer of a posh Toronto hotel. The plight of the solitary aged, some confined to wheelchairs, is relieved on a seven-days-a-week basis by an organization like Meals on Wheels. Some volunteers are told not to wear jewellery nor to carry credit cards or large sums of money with the current climate of violence and theft. The elderly and infirm they serve have to deal with these conditions every day of their lives, and sometimes, even on Christmas, they are too frightened to open their doors, and they remain unfed. What they might miss just as much is the conversation provided by the volunteers as they help them with their meals.

I am haunted by the memory of a sin of omission I committed when I was living in Bristol, England, in 1953. I was rehearsing a musical that was to open on Christmas Day, and every day as I went to rehearsal, I was aware of an old woman who lived alone across the road from me in a makeshift kind of shelter. The winter was unusually severe, but she seemed to wear a perpetual smile.

I kept telling myself that the thing she would like most of all for Christmas was very likely some money to buy food and fuel. Because the show in which I was involved opened on Christmas Day, I didn't seem to find the time to do anything about this. So I was determined to give the money as a kind of Boxing Day present. I had never spoken to the woman, and I'm not even sure that she was capable of speech, but her smile reminded me a bit of my own mom back in Canada.

their private Christmas to share with the down-and-out. The care, however, is still institutional, not unlike Christmas in a barracks. Christmas is the festival of the hearth and home. Most hostels must turn out their temporary guests early enough on Christmas morning so that breakfast can be cleared away and cleaning done and preparations made for the Christmas meal. The meal is usually turkey, sometimes roast beef, and it always includes a gift bag with candy, socks, a scarf, gloves or a tuque. To some homeless men Christmas simply represents a day on which they cannot get any temporary work. Every homeless person who walks the streets on Christmas Day must have a memory of a family celebration in the past. If he or she walks past homes where celebrations are taking place, the

The weather turned bitterly cold on Christmas Day. I came home from the theatre that night, very late, because our cast had had its own belated Christmas party. Since it was too late for a bus, I walked home. I remember going past the Harveys Bristol Cream sherry distillery and savouring the aroma. I inhaled deeply and was rewarded by a kind of contact high. When I finally got home, I was startled to see an ambulance and a police car in front of my lodgings. They were placing a body in the ambulance, but the orders given were to take it to the morgue. The police were very businesslike. They seemed quite abrupt when I questioned them about what had happened: "No coal in her bucket. Poor old sod froze to death."

PART 31

➤ *A surprise visit from Charlie Claus, Santa's lesser-known brother, includes a retelling of one of our most beloved stories. Charlie has a style all his own . . .*

Charlie's
Chrissmuss
Story

BY CHARLIE FARQUHARSON

town, not too much goin' on in yer off-seezin witch at that time took place twelve munths of the yeer. But now that it wuz Tax Time, the Standing Room Only sign wuz up at yer lokel High Holiday Inn. Wen a yung cupple frum Nazzereth tryed to register, and her expeckin' a baby, they wuz tole the oney thing left wuz a single with a stall.

Now you mite not of thot that very accommodatin', but us farm peeple know there's lotsa worse places than a barn fer to bed down at nite. Fer one thing all that hay and straw keeps things warm, and them hevvy draft animals gives off quite a bit of heet too . . . sorta yer bullwarks agin the cold.

And they needed the warmth lemme tell yuh. You mite think it's a topical country out there in yer Middle Eest . . . but you take them sheep herds workin' the nite shift out in yer suberbs . . . I wooden blame them fer to find any eggscuse fer to pull up sheep and spend the nite in town. So you kin jist bet wen they seen the sky fulla lit-up Angles they jist natcherly hi-tailed it outa there, speshully wen they herd them Angles up in the sky singin' yer Hallolulu Chorus.

And sure enuff, that buncha sheepherders found in a little out-bildin backa the hoetell wat the cheef Archy-Angle told them to expeck . . . the one little Person who wuz born to save us all, lyin' in a feed-box wrap up in squabbling close. Uther peeple cum to see Him, too. Three star-struck fellas frum yer further East who had walked menny a mile with ther cammel. They brung Him sum far-out presents: gold, and murr, and insents and franks. That mite not seem too koasher, but they jist worshipt that little baby.

Other hy-mucky-mucks wuz interested too, like yer horrid King Harrid, but fer the rong reesins. Harrid wuz out fer blood cuz he figgered he mite lose his job, and that little baby's pairents hadda take refuse in Eejippt, on the tuther side of yer Sue-us Canal.

And it's all on accounta that little Baby that we are still celibating His Berthday today, cuz He wuz, and still is, God's Chrissmuss present to evry one of us.

W HOSE BIRTHDAY IS IT ANYWAYS? I THINK sumtimes we fergit the most important Person of all this time a year. It's HIS birthday, and WE git all the presents! But then, that's the kind of Person HE always wuz.

Mind you, nobuddy ever called it Chrissmuss the day HE wuz born, way back in yer Roaming Umpires at the beginnins of yer New Testamint. Them Roamuns all called it Income Tax time, and you hadda go back to yer hometown and pay up, persnal delivery.

The place where Our Lord wuz born wuz kind of a one-mule

And to all a good night